First World War
and Army of Occupation
War Diary
France, Belgium and Germany

29 DIVISION
Divisional Troops
510 (1/2 London) Field Company Royal Engineers
1 July 1916 - 28 October 1919

WO95/2293/3

The Naval & Military Press Ltd
www.nmarchive.com
Published in association with The National Archives

Published by

The Naval & Military Press Ltd

Unit 10 Ridgewood Industrial Park,

Uckfield, East Sussex,

TN22 5QE England

Tel: +44 (0) 1825 749494

www.naval-military-press.com

www.nmarchive.com

This diary has been reprinted in facsimile from the original. Any imperfections are inevitably reproduced and the quality may fall short of modern type and cartographic standards.

Contents

Document type	Place/Title	Date From	Date To
Heading	WO95/2293/3 510 (1/2 London) Field Company Royal Artillery		
Heading	29th Division Divl Engineers 1-2nd (London) Fld Coy. E (Jly 1916-Jan 1917) Later 510th (London) Fld Coy R.E. Feb 1917 Oct 1919 1916 July-1919 Oct		
Heading	29th Divisional Engineers 1/2nd London Field Company R.E. July 1916		
Heading	War Diary of 1/2nd London Field Company R.E. (T.F.) From 1st To 31st July 1916 Volume		
War Diary		01/07/1916	27/07/1916
Heading	29th Divisional Engineers 1/2nd London Field Company R.E. August 1916		
War Diary		01/08/1916	31/08/1916
Heading	29th Divisional Engineers 1/2nd London Field Company R.E. September 1916		
War Diary	BEF		
Heading	29th Divisional Engineers 1/2nd London Field Company R.E. October 1916		
War Diary		01/10/1916	31/10/1916
Heading	29th Divisional Engineers 1/2nd London Field Company R.E. November 1916		
War Diary	B.E.F.	01/11/1916	30/11/1916
Heading	29th Divisional Engineers 1/2nd London Field Company R.E. December 1916		
Heading	War Diary of 1/2nd London Field Company R.E.T. From December 1st 1916 To December 31st 1916 (Volume 1)		
War Diary	B.E.F.	01/12/1916	31/12/1916
Heading	War Diary of 510 1/2nd London Field Company R.E (T) From January 1st 1917 To January 31st 1917 (Volume 1)		
War Diary	B.E.F.	01/01/1917	31/01/1917
Heading	War Diary of 510th (London) Field Co., R.E. (T.F.) For Month Of February, 1917. Volume III		
War Diary	B.E.F.	01/02/1917	28/02/1917
Heading	War Diary of 510th (London) Field Co., R.E. From 1st March, 1917 To 31st March, 1917 (Volume I)		
War Diary	B.E.F.	01/03/1917	31/03/1917
Heading	War Diary of 510th (London) Field Co., R.E. From 1st April, 1917 To 30th April, 1917. Volume X		
War Diary	B.E.F.	01/04/1917	30/04/1917
Heading	War Diary of 510 (London) Field Company R.E. From 1st Of May 1917 To 31st May 1917 Volume I Part II		
War Diary	B.E.F.	01/05/1917	31/05/1917
War Diary	War Diary of 510th (London) Field Co., R.E. From 1st June, 1917. To 30th June. 1917 Volume XII		
War Diary	B.E.F.	01/06/1917	30/06/1917
Heading	War Diary of 510th (London) Field Company R.E. From 1st July, 1917 To 30th July, 1917. Volume XIII		
War Diary	B.E.F.	01/07/1917	31/07/1917

Heading	War Diary of 510th (London) Field Company R.E. From 1st August, 1917 To 31st August, 1917. Volume XIV		
War Diary	B.E.F.	01/08/1917	30/08/1917
Heading	War Diary of 510th (London) Field Company R.E. From 1st September, 1917. To 30th September, 1917. Volume XV		
War Diary	B.E.F.	01/09/1917	30/09/1917
Heading	War Diary of 510th (London) Field Company R.E. From 1st October, 1917, To 31st October, 1917. Volume XVI		
War Diary	B.E.F.	01/10/1917	31/10/1917
Heading	War Diary of 510th (London) Field Coy., R.E., Volume 17. (November 1917)		
Heading	War Diary of 510th (London) Field Company R.E. Volume 17		
War Diary	B.E.F.	01/11/1917	30/11/1917
Heading	War Diary of 510th (London) Field Coy. R.E. From December 1st To December 31st 1917 (Volume 18)		
War Diary	B.E.F.	01/12/1917	31/01/1918
War Diary	B.E.F.	27/01/1918	31/01/1918
Diagram etc	Sketch Plan Of Drainage Divl Reserve Line S Gravenstafel		
Heading	War Diary of 510th (London) Field Coy R.E. From 1/2/18 To 28/2/18 Volume XIX		
War Diary	B.E.F.	01/02/1918	28/02/1918
War Diary		27/02/1918	27/02/1918
Heading	War Diary of 510th (London) Field Coy. R.E. From 1-3-18 To 31-3-18 Volume No 21		
War Diary	B.E.F.	01/03/1918	31/03/1918
Heading	29th Divisional Engineers 510th (London) Field Company R.E. April 1918		
Heading	War Diary of 510th (London) Field Coy. R.E. From 1/4/18 To 30/4/18 Volume 22		
War Diary	B.E.F.	01/04/1918	30/04/1918
Heading	War Diary of 510th (London) Fd Coy R.E. From 1/5/18 To 31/5/18 Volume XXIII		
War Diary	B.E.F.	01/05/1918	31/05/1918
Heading	War Diary of 510th (London) Field Coy, R.E. From 1/6/18 To 30/6/18 Volume 24		
War Diary	B.E.F.	01/06/1918	30/06/1918
Heading	War Diary of 510th (London) Field Coy R.E. From 1.7.18 To 31.7.18 Volume 25		
War Diary	B.E.F.	01/07/1918	31/07/1918
Miscellaneous	570th Field Coy. R.E. Company Scheme	11/07/1918	11/07/1918
Miscellaneous	Map Ref Sheet 36 A. 1,40,000		
Miscellaneous	O.C. No. 1 Section		
Miscellaneous	O.C. No. 21 Section		
Miscellaneous	O.C. No. 3 Section		
Miscellaneous	O.C. No. 4 Section		
Miscellaneous	Company Scheme General Idea	16/07/1918	16/07/1918
Miscellaneous	O.C. No. 1 Section		
Miscellaneous	O.C. No. 2 Section		
Miscellaneous	O.C. No. 3 Section		
Miscellaneous	O.C. No. 4 Section		

Heading	War Diary of 510th (London) Field Coy. R.E. Volume 26 From 1-8-18 To 31-8-18		
War Diary	B.E.F.	01/08/1918	31/08/1918
Operation(al) Order(s)	Movement Order No. 6. 510th (London) Field Company R.E.	22/08/1918	22/08/1918
Operation(al) Order(s)	510th. Field Coy. R.E. Movement Order No. 7	24/08/1918	24/08/1918
Operation(al) Order(s)	510th. (London) Field Coy. R.E. Movement Order No. 8	31/08/1918	31/08/1918
Heading	War Diary of 510th (London) Field Coy. R.E. From 1-9-1918 To 30-9-18 Volume 27		
War Diary	B.E.F.	01/09/1918	30/09/1918
Operation(al) Order(s)	510th Field Company R.E. Movement Order No. 10	19/09/1918	19/09/1918
Operation(al) Order(s)	510th Field Coy R.E. Movement Order No. 11	21/09/1918	21/09/1918
Miscellaneous	List Of Material At Dumps. On Evening Of 22-9-18	22/09/1918	22/09/1918
Operation(al) Order(s)	510th. Field Company R.E. Operation Order No. 3	23/09/1918	23/09/1918
Miscellaneous	510th. Field Company R.E. Administrative Instructions No. 3	24/09/1918	24/09/1918
Miscellaneous	510th. Field Coy. R.E. Addendum To Adminintrative Order No. 3		
Miscellaneous	510th. Field Company R.E. Addendum To Operation Order No. 3	26/09/1918	26/09/1918
Operation(al) Order(s)	510th Field Company R.E. Movement Order No. 12	26/09/1918	26/09/1918
Heading	War Diary of 510th (London) Field Coy. R.E. Volume. 28 From 1-10-18 To 31-10-18		
War Diary	B.E.F.	01/10/1918	31/10/1918
Heading	War Diary of 510th (London) Field Coy R.E. From 1-11-18 To 30-11-18 Volume 29		
War Diary	B.E.F.	01/11/1918	30/11/1918
Heading	War Diary of 510th (London) Field Coy. R.E. From 1-12-18 To 31-12-18 Volume No 30		
War Diary	B.E.F.	01/12/1918	31/12/1918
Heading	Rhine Army Southern Division Late 29th Division 510th (London) Fld Coy R.E. Jan-Oct 1919		
Heading	War Diary of 510th Field Coy R.E From 1/1/19 To 31/1/19 Volume No 30		
War Diary	Burscheid Germany	01/01/1919	31/01/1919
Heading	War Diary of 510th (London) Field Coy R.E. Volume 32 From 1-2-19 To 28-2-19		
War Diary	Burscheid Germany	01/02/1919	28/02/1919
Heading	War Diary of 510th London Field Coy. R.E. From May 1st To May 31st Volume No 35		
War Diary		01/05/1919	29/05/1919
Heading	War Diary For June 510 London Field Coy. R.E. Volume No 36		
War Diary	Burscheid Germany	01/06/1919	29/06/1919
Heading	War Diary of 510th London Field Company R.E.		
War Diary	Burscheid Germany	01/07/1919	28/07/1919
Heading	War Diary of 510th London Field Company R.E.		
War Diary	Burscheid	01/08/1919	27/08/1919
Heading	War Diary of 510th London Field Company R.E.		
War Diary	Burscheid	01/09/1919	30/09/1919
Heading	War Diary of 510th London Field Company R.E.		
War Diary	Burscheid	01/10/1919	28/10/1919

WO/95/2293

1/3 510 (1/2 London) Field Company
Royal Artillery

29TH DIVISION

DIVL ENGINEERS

1-2ND (LONDON) FLD COY R.E.

(JLY 1916 - JAN 1917)

LATER

510TH (LONDON) FLD COY R.E.

FEB 1917 - ~~[illegible]~~ Oct 1919

1916 July — 1919 Oct

29th Divisional Engineers

1/2nd LONDON FIELD COMPANY R. E.

J U L Y 1 9 1 6

CONFIDENTIAL

121

W A R   D I A R Y

of

1/2nd LONDON FIELD COMPANY R.E.,(T.F.)

from 1st to 31st JULY,1916.

V O L U M E ~~XV~~

Instructions regarding War Diaries and Intelligence Summaries are contained in F. S. Regs., Part II. and the Staff Manual respectively. Title pages will be prepared in manuscript.

WAR DIARY

~~or~~

~~INTELLIGENCE SUMMARY.~~

(Erase heading not required.)

Army Form C. 2118.

1/2nd London Field Co. R.E., (T)

5

Place	Date	Hour	Summary of Events and Information	Remarks and references to Appendices
	1st July		- Company bivouaced near ENGLEBELMER, 500 yards to west at P.24.C.1.1 (Sheet 57D S.E) affiliated to 88th Brigade. No 2539 Sapper Snell, J. showed courage & resource in carrying a message to & bringing an answer from Brigade H.Qs Company dump in ENGLEBELMER. Mounted Section at ACHEUX.	
	3rd		Reported to 87th Brigade, and received orders about taking over new sector - draining, revetting, widening and improving communication trenches.	
	4th		- Company to MARTINSART - commenced sector work.	
	5th		- Company to bivouac Q.31.2.74 (Sheet 57D S.E) near MARTINSART Mounted section joined Company. Carrying up material for wiring, all day, & wired all night - returning between to move kits & get food.	
	5th - 11th		. Wiring in front for new front trench. Nights 5/6, 6/7, 7/8, 9/10 and 10/11. 300 yards beyond front line, starting before digging party - 20 drivers employed on latter two nights. Sergt Higgs specially noticeable for coolness & good work when covering party broke back taking sappers with them on 5/6th. Corpl Willett very cool in charge of 8 remaining, while 2nd Lt. Norris returned for party. Sapper Hitchcock volunteered to accompany OC forward to reconnoitre. Other N.C.Os who showed up well - A/Sgt. Collins, Corp East, Corp Holt, Corp Preston, L/cpl Barnes, L/cpl Gray, L/cpl Bray.	
	11th		- Carrying material for Mill post (in marshes) and wiring at night (E of HAMEL at Q24a63)	
	15th		- Further wiring & consolidating this post until night of 22/23rd when the lower roof of the keep was completed.	

Army Form C. 2118.

6

Instructions regarding War Diaries and Intelligence Summaries are contained in F. S. Regs., Part II. and the Staff Manual respectively. Title pages will be prepared in manuscript.

WAR DIARY
or
~~INTELLIGENCE SUMMARY.~~
(Erase heading not required.)

1/2nd London Field Co. R.E., (T).

Place	Date	Hour	Summary of Events and Information	Remarks and references to Appendices
	July 18th		Taping at night for another new front trench. 2nd Lt. Norris with orderly and A/2nd Cpl Barnes found ball of German tape on our wire - in front of trench only held by posts half a mile apart - with tape leading out from German sap. Pulled in over 200 yards of tape & used it on own work. Interrupted by German patrol. Got post to disperse this with Lewis gun.	
	18/19 to 20/21		Taping & digging communication trenches continued. All officers out at different times on night work, taking turns for day work. The taping being finished by Capt. Ryan on 20/21 & 21/22.	
	21/22		At taping work the following did specially well 18/19 & 19/20 A/2nd Cpl Barnes and Sapper Cox, 20/21 & 21/22 A/2nd Cpl Bray. 20/21 Sapper Hitchcock. 21/22 Sapper Causley.	
	19/20		A/Sgt Collins very cool & resourceful in trying to rally stampeding Infantry working party, Peck St. Extension.	
	20/23		On night of 22nd/23rd forward communication trenches, cleared, & obstacles placed ready for blocking these - in front of old firing line - in case of need. L/Cpl Malin good with infantry party under fire.	
	23rd		Company moved to LOUVENCOURT, ceasing to be affiliated to 86th Brigade & bivouaced, resting.	
	23rd/26th		All details joined the Company	
	27th		Company marched to CANDAS & entrained night 27/28th arriving on morning	

1577 Wt. W10791/1773 500,000 1/15 D. D. & L. A.D.S.S./Forms/C. 2118.

29th Divisional Engineers

1/2nd LONDON FIELD COMPANY R. E.

AUGUST 1 9 1 6

Instructions regarding War Diaries and Intelligence Summaries are contained in F. S. Regs., Part II. and the Staff Manual respectively. Title pages will be prepared in manuscript.

WAR DIARY for August 1916.
or
~~INTELLIGENCE SUMMARY.~~
(Erase heading not required.)

Army Form C. 2118.

1/2nd London Field Co. R.E., (T).

Vol 2

Place	Date	Hour	Summary of Events and Information	Remarks and references to Appendices
	1/8/16		Work at Ypres – Strong points, dug-outs and M.G. Emplacements, and supervising work on main communications and X line – men attached to Infantry for front line work :- Chiefly night work.	
			Work at Camp A 28 d 5.2. – making up trench Stores.	
	2nd to 5th	—	Third section to Ypres – Coming up in 4 detachments. in order to carry out work on Ecole Strong Post. allotted as the principal work of the Company.	
	night 8/9		Gas attack – first experience by the Company – One Sapper, Sapper Lyons, to F. Ambulance, Gas poisoning, having delayed putting on helmet while warning the adj. M.G. Coy + the Infantry working party, working under his supervision. When ordered to Fd Ambulance, he sent back from there a report + sketch of work done during night	
	to 31st.		Remainder of month, work as detailed on 1st of month.	
			One section at Camp, remainder forward, one being relieved each week.	

W. Mance [signature]
Major RE
1-9-16
O.C. 1/2 London Fd. Co. RE

29th Divisional Engineers

1/2nd LONDON FIELD COMPAMY R. E.

SEPTEMBER 1 9 1 6

Army Form C. 2118.

Instructions regarding War Diaries and Intelligence Summaries are contained in F. S. Regs., Part II. and the Staff Manual respectively. Title pages will be prepared in manuscript.

WAR DIARY of 1/2nd London Field Co. R.E., (T).

~~or~~

~~INTELLIGENCE SUMMARY.~~ FOR SEPTEMBER 1916.

(Erase heading not required.)

Vol 3

Place	Date	Hour	Summary of Events and Information	Remarks and references to Appendices
BEF			Company distribution as for August – 3 sections at Ypres, 1 section changed weekly. HQ + Mounted Section at Camp A 28 d 5.2 near Poperinghe. Principal work – École strong post, chiefly elephant shelters, and new duck walk trench.	

[signature] 30-9-16
MAJOR R.E.
O/C 1/2nd London Field Co. R.E., (T).

29th Divisional Engineers

1/2nd LONDON FIELD COMPANY R. E.

OCTOBER 1 9 1 6

1 PAGE 1

Instructions regarding War Diaries and Intelligence Summaries are contained in F. S. Regs., Part II. and the Staff Manual respectively. Title pages will be prepared in manuscript.

WAR DIARY for OCTOBER 1916
~~or~~
~~**INTELLIGENCE SUMMARY.**~~ of 1/2ND LONDON FLD COY R.E.T.
(Erase heading not required.)

Vol 4

Army Form C. 2118.

Place	Date	Hour	Summary of Events and Information	Remarks and references to Appendices
	1 10/16		Company distribution as for September. 3 Sections at Ypres - 1 section changed weekly. 1 Section H.Q + Mounted Section at Camp A 28 d 5/2 near POPERINGHE. YPRES detachment withdrawn on 3rd 4th .5th Principal Work :— Ecole Strong Point - Elephant Shelters + screens. Causeways across BELLEVARDE BEKE (Completed). Putting M.G. emplacements in order, including new concrete one in F/5 near MENIN ROAD (completed)	
	5 10/16		Company marched to HOUTKERQUE, arrived 17.30 went into Billets. Warned that Corps commander would inspect R.E. Coys next day	
	6 10/16		29th Divisional Engineers (less Signal Coy) inspected by VIII Corps Commander Company present less Headquarter Section of mounted portion.	
	7 10/16		Marched to PROVEN (VIA WATEAU) Parade 22-30 Commenced entraining at Proven Railhead at 54 minutes past midnight. Tea made for men before departure at 3-20 am.	
	8 10/16		Train journey to SALEUX, S.W. OF AMIENS - no stop for meals or watering horses - via HAZEBROUKE, ST. OMER, CALAIS, BOULOGNE and ABBEVILLE. Detrained at 1800. Took horses a mile to water + made tea for men. Marched off at 2100 to CORBIE via AMIENS, 15 miles.	
	9 10/16		Coy arrived approximately at 4.30 am. and got into dirty billets at the	

1577 Wt. W10791/1773 500,000 1/15 D. D. & L. A.D.S.S./Forms/C. 2118.

Army Form C. 2118.

Instructions regarding War Diaries and Intelligence Summaries are contained in F. S. Regs., Part II. and the Staff Manual respectively. Title pages will be prepared in manuscript.

WAR DIARY
or
INTELLIGENCE SUMMARY.

(*Erase heading not required.*)

Place	Date	Hour	Summary of Events and Information	Remarks and references to Appendices
	9th Contd.		Chateau near the Square. Field allotted for horse lines almost belly deep in mud at approaches + standings very muddy. Company attached with Brigade to 12th Division 15th Corps.	
	10/10/16		Paraded at 0800 to follow Brigade en route to POMMIER REDOUBT. arrived at bivouac at 1900 – 12 miles –.	
	11/10/16		Marched from bivouac to West Side of BERNAFAY WOOD, to bivouac there. – O/C + 2 section officers made reconnaissance of front line	
	12/10/16		O/C + four officers each with a section of 1 N.C.O. + 18 Sappers left bivouac at 0830 to take up position in Goat trench E. of GUEUDECOURT in readiness for consolidation after assault by 88th Brigade in conjunction with 12th Division	
	12/13		One section connected right of Brigade to next Brigade. One section improved newly taken front line trench. Other two sections re-opened old + constructed new communication trenches up to new front line.	
	13th to 17th		Two sections each night on improving front line trench + strong posts on left flank – flank in air.	
	18th to 19th		Two sections, one to a strong post on each flank of Brigade – newly taken trench – left flank being in the air. Right flank section sniped at a good deal, left section, flank in air, manned newly made post and	

1577 Wt. W10791/1773 500,000 1/15 D. D. & L. A.D.S.S./Forms/C. 2118.

Instructions regarding War Diaries and Intelligence Summaries are contained in F. S. Regs., Part II. and the Staff Manual respectively. Title pages will be prepared in manuscript.

WAR DIARY
or
INTELLIGENCE SUMMARY.
(Erase heading not required.)

Army Form C. 2118.

Place	Date	Hour	Summary of Events and Information	Remarks and references to Appendices
			repulsed enemy bombing party, approach noticed + alarm given by Sergt. Collins. Work after successful attack by 88th Brigade – attached 12th Division – North of GUEUDECOURT.	
	20/10/16		Company ceased to be affiliated to Brigade (gone into Divl Reserve) for work + with the Brigade ceased to be attached to the 12th Division, returning to 29th Division, its own division. When in the line Nos 3 + 4 Sections did the best work, + the most important – ii Lts Norris (No 3) + Standen (No 4). All the Section sergeants showed up specially well – Sergts. Higgs, Collins East + Holt – also the undermentioned:– 2nd Corpl. (now acting Corpl.) – Barnes; L/ce Corpl. (now acting ii Corpl.) Steadman; Sappers Catton, Standen + Walker (now L/c unpaid)	
	20th to 29th		Camp not moved. Work chiefly on LONGUEVAL – FLERS Road, with 1/1 W Riding Fld Coy R.E.T. – Major Baylay as senior officer Cdg. in charge of this work. Other works – Erection of shelters for 88th Brigade – huts, elephants, + tarpaulins (ii Lt Wainwright) – Supervision, earth road MONTAUBAN TO LONGUEVAL – Reconnaissance, marking out + making practicable pack track BERNAFAY TO BAZENTIN + on from junction at LONGUEVAL to FLERS (ii Lt Williamson). Reconnaissance of GUEUDECOURT for wells (ii Lt P. Hay).	
	30th		Relieved by 3rd Australian Fld Coy + marched to MAMETZ VILLAGE (huts) F5c 44. roofing four huts for our occupation	
	31 Oct		Marched to TREUX.	

W Macrae Major R.E. 1-11-16
O.C. 1/2 London Fd. Co. R.E. T

1577 Wt. W10791/1773 500,000 1/15 D. D. & L. A.D.S.S./Forms/C. 2118.

29th Divisional Engineers

1/2nd LONDON FIELD COMPANY R. E.

NOVEMBER A1 9 1 6

Vol ~~4~~ 5 ~~Army~~ Form C. 2118.

Instructions regarding War Diaries and Intelligence Summaries are contained in F. S. Regs., Part II. and the Staff Manual respectively. Title pages will be prepared in manuscript.

WAR DIARY FOR NOVEMBER 1916 or ~~INTELLIGENCE SUMMARY.~~ OF 1/2ND LONDON FIELD CO. R.E.T.

(Erase heading not required.)

Place	Date	Hour	Summary of Events and Information	Remarks and references to Appendices
B.E.F.	1/11/16 to 11/11/16		At TREUX Building Brigade stables + standings.	
	12/11/16		Marched to MEAULTE less one section left on stables.	
	13/11/16		Marched to MANSEL CAMP do.	
	13/11/16 to 16/11/16		Attached to GUARDS Division. Working under C.E. XIV Corps on MANSEL Camp. (Nissen Bow Huts.)	
	16/11/16		Section from TREUX rejoined Company.	
	17/11/16		Marched to GUILLEMONT, rejoining 88th Brigade, camping beside Bde H.Q. in half sunk shelters taken over from 2nd Field Coy R.E. Mounted Section camped on East side of BERNAFAY WOOD.	
	17/11/16 to end of Month		Work – Duckwalk 2 days. FLERS Line. Carpenters work on mined dug-outs for Field Artillery. Advanced Dressing Station, GINCHY. Notice Boards, Box Latrines &c for Bde including transporting + arranging material.	
	23/11/16		Two Sections moved to new Company Camp at S 30. a 7 5.	
	24/11/16		Third Section moved to same Camp.	
	25/11/16		H.Q. + remaining Section moved to same camp.	
	24/11/16		New left sector Duckwalk commenced.	
	29/11/16		Started work on OZONE ALLEY + on Battalion Camp GUILLEMONT. Ceased work on FLERS LINE.	

1577 Wt. W10791/1773 500,000 1/15 D. D. & L. A.D.S.S./Forms/C. 2118.

CONTINUED TO PAGE 2.

Army Form C. 2118.

Instructions regarding War Diaries and Intelligence Summaries are contained in F. S. Regs., Part II. and the Staff Manual respectively. Title pages will be prepared in manuscript.

WAR DIARY for NOVEMBER 1916 or ~~INTELLIGENCE SUMMARY.~~ of 1/2nd LONDON FIELD Co. R.E.T.

(Erase heading not required.)

Place	Date	Hour	Summary of Events and Information	Remarks and references to Appendices
	30/11/16		Mounted Section moved from Camp beside BERNAFAY WOOD + joined the Company at S.30.a.7.5. Honours received during the month:- No 1178 2/Corporal GRAY. T. - Silver Star of SERBIA (for GALLIPOLI) No 1098 Sergeant COLLINS. J. - Military Medal - for gallantry NORTH of GUEUDECOURT on night of 18th/19th October. W. Macrae Major RE 30-11-16 O.C. 1/2 London Fd Co. R.E.T	

1577 Wt. W10791/1773 500,000 1/15 D. D. & L. A.D.S.S./Forms/C. 2118.

29th Divisional Engineers

1/2nd LONDON FIELD COMPAMY R. E.

DECEMBER 1 9 1 6

Vol. 6

CONFIDENTIAL.

WAR DIARY

OF

1/2ND LONDON FIELD COMPANY R.E.T.

FROM DECEMBER 1ST 1916 TO DECEMBER 31ST 1916.

(VOLUME 1.)

BW

Army Form C. 2118.

Instructions regarding War Diaries and Intelligence Summaries are contained in F. S. Regs., Part II. and the Staff Manual respectively. Title pages will be prepared in manuscript.

WAR DIARY OF 1/2ND LONDON FIELD COY. R.E.T. ~~or INTELLIGENCE SUMMARY.~~ FOR MONTH OF DECEMBER 1916.

(Erase heading not required.)

Place	Date	Hour	Summary of Events and Information	Remarks and references to Appendices
B.E.F.	1 12/16 to 9 12/16		In Camp near TRONES WOOD at S.30 a.7.5.	
			Work at GUILLEMONT & between GINCHY & LESBOEUFS chiefly -	
			GUILLEMONT Camp - Elephant shelters erected for 2 Battalions in conjunction with 1/1st W. Riding 7th. Coy R.E.	
			GINCHY Advanced Dressing Station - Completed required improvements.	
			OZONE AVENUE - Digging up trench boards & fixing on trestles	
			Left Sector Duckwalk, Mined M.G. Dug-outs, Relay Post (Mined Dug-out), Artillery Mined Dug-outs.	
	night 8th 9th		Engineering superintendence of two strong posts in front of OX & COW trenches.	
	10th		Marched to CITADEL Camp.	
	11th		Marched to CORBIE, picking up pontoon & bridge equipment & bicycles at MEAULTE.	
	12th		No 1 Section marched to DAOURS to work on the 29th Divisional School.	
			Pontoons, bridge equipment & bicycles left at DAOURS.	
			Mounted Section marched to LONGPRE.	
			Company entrained at CORBIE, detrained at HANGEST & marched to FOURDRINOY.	
	13th		Changed all billets; the first ones were the only ones available & were bad.	
			Mounted section arrived at FOURDRINOY.	
	17th		Company, less No 1 Section, marched to LE QUESNOY.	

1577 Wt. W10791/1773 500,000 1/15 D. D. & L. A.D.S.S./Forms/C. 2118.

CONTINUED TO PAGE 2.

Instructions regarding War Diaries and Intelligence Summaries are contained in F. S. Regs., Part II. and the Staff Manual respectively. Title pages will be prepared in manuscript.

WAR DIARY OF 1/2ND LONDON FIELD COY. R.E.T. or INTELLIGENCE SUMMARY. FOR MONTH OF DECEMBER 1916 (CONTD.)

Army Form C. 2118.

(Erase heading not required.)

Place	Date	Hour	Summary of Events and Information	Remarks and references to Appendices
B. E. 7.	21 12/16		Company bathed at RIENCOURT.	
	22nd		No 4 Section marched to FLIXÉCOURT to work on the Fourth Army School of Instruction.	
	13th to 31st		Company in Rest Area employed in training + re-equipping.	
			W Macrae Major RE 31-12-16	

Vol 7

CONFIDENTIAL

WAR DIARY

OF

510 1/2ND LONDON FIELD COMPANY R.E.(T.)

FROM: JANUARY 1ST 1917 TO: JANUARY 31ST 1917

(VOLUME 1.)

Instructions regarding War Diaries and Intelligence Summaries are contained in F. S. Regs., Part II. and the Staff Manual respectively. Title pages will be prepared in manuscript.

WAR DIARY of 1/2nd London Field Coy. R.E.(T.)

~~or~~

~~INTELLIGENCE SUMMARY.~~ for Month of January 1917.

(Erase heading not required.)

Army Form C. 2118.

Place	Date	Hour	Summary of Events and Information	Remarks and references to Appendices
B.E.F.	1/1/17		Company at LE QUESNOY, in rest area training & re-equipping. No 4 Section at FLIXECOURT works for Army School. No 1 Section at DAOURS works for all the Schools there.	
	8/1/17		No. 4 Section rejoined Company at LE QUESNOY by motor bus.	
			Transport marched to AILLY-SUR-SOMME, No 4 Section Transport joining the Company Transport there.	
	9/1/17		Company (less No 1 Section) marched to PICQUIGNY & went on by motor lorry to DAOURS. No 1 Section joining the Company there.	
	10/1/17		Transport marched to DAOURS & re-joined the Company.	
	10/1/17 to 12/1/17		Pontooning - all three Divisional R.E. Companies working together. Company also continued work in DAOURS.	
	13/1/17		Advance party sent on.	
			Company marched to MEAULTE.	
	14/1/17		Company marched to old camp near TRONES WOOD at S.30.a.7.5 & completed relief of 78th Field Coy. R.E. there.	
	14/1/17 to 20/1/17		Work:- GINCHY Duckwalk Loop - linked through GINCHY-LESBOEUFS Road & Mule Track. OX TRENCH - Revetting or trench boarding on trestles after clearing - way made passable from Duck-Walk to Sunk Road.	
	NIGHT 21st/22nd		Dug front line trench in conjunction with 1/1st West Riding Field Coy R.E. & 1/2nd Monmouth Pioneers. Thanked for work by G.O.C. Division - Company 100 strong on work, besides medical orderly & stretcher bearers, with C.S.M. Bowles, ii Lieuts. Wainwright & Harden & O.C. Paraded 3 p.m., arrived back 3.15 a.m.	

1577 Wt. W10791/1773 500,000 1/15 D. D. & L. A.D.S.S./Forms/C. 2118.

CONTINUED TO PAGE 2

Army Form C. 2118.

Instructions regarding War Diaries and Intelligence Summaries are contained in F. S. Regs., Part II. and the Staff Manual respectively. Title pages will be prepared in manuscript.

WAR DIARY of 1/2ND LONDON FIELD COY. R.E.(T) ~~or INTELLIGENCE SUMMARY.~~ FOR MONTH OF JANUARY 1917.

(Erase heading not required.)

Place	Date	Hour	Summary of Events and Information	Remarks and references to Appendices
B.E.F.	24/1/17		Continued work on GINCHY-LESBOEUFS road + on doubling GINCHY Duckwalk loop.	
			Commenced clearing + bunking GUILLEMONT Camp	
			Carted German knife rests + barbed wire from COMBLES to HAIE WOOD R.E. Dump under Artillery fire. (Mounted) L/Cpl (Acting ii Cpl.) Snow did conspicuously good work in charge of transport + loading under Capt. Ryan.	
	night 24th/25th		In conjunction with 1/1st West Riding Field Coy. both under O.C. 1/2 London Field Coy. + each having 100 Monmouth Pioneers as carriers, laid out between 150 + 160 knife rests round front line salient. London Coy. round actual salient. W. Riding Coy. on left. Had artillery casualties on way up. Paraded 2 p.m., arrived back 11.15 p.m. Company 80 strong on work besides stretcher bearers + ii Lieutenants Williamson + May.	
			Conspicuous for good work Sergts. Higgs + Collins, Sappers Catton + Dancer	
	26/1/17		Work as for 24th.	
	night 27th/28th		Wiring newly captured position, with 87th Bde. Sapping Platoons as carriers.	
			Sergt. Holt, being with a party that was returning owing to heavy enemy barrage, hearing that the other party out wiring had suffered heavy casualties including the Officer (Actually 1 Officer + 9 O.R. all wounded) volunteered to go to help it, + eventually saw all the wounded in, giving valuable assistance to Sergt. Higgs of this party.	
	night 28th/29th		Two sections under ii Lieut. Wainwright with two sections of 1/1st West Riding Fld. Coy. R.E.T under ii Lieut. Lane, all under Capt. Ryan wiring front line.	
			Sergts. Collins + Holt showed determination, intelligence + gallantry when reconnoitering to right flank to make connection with next post, until they eventually met Lieut. Lyne	

CONTINUED TO PAGE 3

WAR DIARY of 1/2ND LONDON FIELD COY. R.E.(T)
~~or~~
~~INTELLIGENCE SUMMARY.~~ FOR MONTH OF JANUARY 1917.

(Erase heading not required.)

Instructions regarding War Diaries and Intelligence Summaries are contained in F. S. Regs., Part II. and the Staff Manual respectively. Title pages will be prepared in manuscript.

Army Form C. 2118.

Place	Date	Hour	Summary of Events and Information	Remarks and references to Appendices
B.E.F.			who had lost his way – who was close to the enemy line under fire from snipers.	
			Sergts. Holt + Collins + Corpl. Collingwood were conspicuous for good work.	
	night 29th/30th		Similar work to former night – under Major Macrae. Sections under 2 Lieuts. Williamson + Gurney. – 2 Lieut. Wainwright + Sergt. Collins laid a tape from sunk road post to traversed trench post.	
			London casualties 12 wounded, 6 slightly wounded: all brought in.	
			175 yards wiring done.	
			Sapper Begley + Corpl. Collingwood (slightly wounded, at duty) were conspicuous for good work. The men, including the 10 drivers carrying wire, very steady under rather heavy fire with corresponding casualties.	
	night 30th/31st		Similar work to former night – under Major Wilson R.E. 1/1st W. Riding Field Coy. R.E.T.	
			2 Lieut. Harden's party did good work; Sergt. Holt armed with bombs, went out + took prisoners 3 of the 119th Grenadier Regt. seen by him in front of the wire.	
			2 Lieut. Williamson's party failed to do any wiring owing to heavy shelling.	
			Sergt. Holt was conspicuous for good work also Corporal Barnes.	
			Change in designation of Company.	
			Authority W.O. letter No 9/Engineers/7611 (A.G.7) of 6-1-17.	
			From February 1st 1917 this Company is to be known as the:	
			510th (LONDON) FIELD COMPANY. R.E.	

1577 Wt. W10791/1773 500,000 1/15 D. D. & L. A.D.S.S./Forms/C. 2118.

CONTINUED TO PAGE 4.

Instructions regarding War Diaries and Intelligence Summaries are contained in F. S. Regs., Part II. and the Staff Manual respectively. Title pages will be prepared in manuscript.

WAR DIARY OF 1/2ND LONDON FIELD COY R.E.T. ~~or INTELLIGENCE SUMMARY.~~ FOR MONTH OF JANUARY 1917.

(Erase heading not required.)

Army Form C. 2118.

Place	Date	Hour	Summary of Events and Information	Remarks and references to Appendices
B.E.F.			Honours received during the month :-	
			Lieut P.H. THORNE / No 1238 Sergt. E.H. HIGGS } Mentioned in Despatches. Supplement of London Gazette War Office 2-1-17.	
			Former Honours :	
			From 18-3-15 to commencement of Diary 1-7-16.	
			" Lieut A.O LAIRD - Military Cross - London Gazette of 8-11-15.	
			No 103 Sergt. J COX (Killed) / No 1545 Sapper J. GODWYN } Mentioned in Despatches. for Gallipoli Peninsula 12-7-15.	
			Notified by 29th Divl. Engrs. H.Q. Gazette not given.	
			No 406 C.S.M. C. BOWLES - D.C.M.	
			"For conspicuous gallantry when employed in wiring under heavy fire. He set a fine example".	
			London Gazette of 17th May 1916.	
			Notified by 29th Divl Engrs H.Q. as for period 24th Aug to 31st Oct. 1915.	
			No 406 C.S.M. C. BOWLES. - Mentioned in Despatches 28-1-16. London Gazette 5-5-16 (No 29541.)	
			" Lieut P.H. THORNE. - Mentioned in Despatches. London Gazette No 29541 of 10-4-16.	
			" Lieut. F.C. HOLLAND. - Croix de Guerre in 1915. Reference not now traceable.	

CONTINUED TO PAGE 5

Instructions regarding War Diaries and Intelligence Summaries are contained in F. S. Regs., Part II. and the Staff Manual respectively. Title pages will be prepared in manuscript.

WAR DIARY OF 1/2ND LONDON FIELD COY. R.E.T. ~~or INTELLIGENCE SUMMARY.~~ FOR MONTH OF JANUARY 1917.

(*Erase heading not required.*)

Army Form C. 2118.

Place	Date	Hour	Summary of Events and Information	Remarks and references to Appendices
B.E.F.			Notes on Organisation, Equipment &c. Royal Engineers have to work to a great extent with Infantry. It would be advantageous if the organisation corresponded more to that of Infantry, for instance if a section were enlarged to platoon strength. This is especially the case as regards N.C.Os + their ranks. Stripes add greatly to the efficiency of any man when giving technical assistance to Infantry or when dealing with carrying parties. Especially Infantry do not understand the rank "Second Corporal" + that it is senior to Lance Corporal, but take it to be the same rank. It would be an advantage if 2nd Corpls. were called Corporals - on the present pay of " Corporals - + if Corporals were called Lance Sergeants - on the present pay of Corporals. [illegible] Major R.E. 31-1-17 O.C. 1/2 London Fd. Coy R.E.T.	

Vol 8

War Diary

of

510th (London) Field Co.,R.E. (T.F.)

for Month of February,1917.

Volume III

Instructions regarding War Diaries and Intelligence Summaries are contained in F. S. Regs., Part II. and the Staff Manual respectively. Title pages will be prepared in manuscript.

WAR DIARY OF 510TH LONDON FIELD COY. R.E.

~~INTELLIGENCE SUMMARY.~~ FOR MONTH OF FEBRUARY 1917.

(Erase heading not required.)

Army Form C. 2118.

Place	Date	Hour	Summary of Events and Information	Remarks and references to Appendices
B.E.F.	1ST		Location - Camp at S.30.a.7.5. near TRONES WOOD - camp originally built by the company. Morning - Completed doubling of GINCHY Duckwalk Loop + continued flooring of GUILLEMONT Camp elephant shelters.	
	night 1st/2nd		In conjunction with 455th (West Riding) Fld. Coy. R.E. continued wiring operations in LESBOEUFS Sector, with 100 Pioneers, ½ Monmouths carrying to advanced R.E. dump + 100 Infantry from 87th Bde. Sapping platoons carrying forward to advanced dumps - work under Major Macrae.	
			Notification from C.R.E. that the G.O.C. considered it a good nights work + the report (which included reconnaissance) a very valuable one + did not propose calling upon the R.E. to do any more wiring.	
			The Company's casualties during the wiring operations were: Killed. 2 other ranks. Wounded 2 officers + 25 other ranks. Slightly wounded at duty 11 other ranks.	
			On the night 31st January-1st February there was no wiring as the Corps Commander requested the G.O.C. Divn. to give the R.E. a night off on account of the good work done on wiring by them. On the 31st January G.O.C. Divn. also sent through the C.R.E. his appreciation of the good work carried out in spite of hostile fire.	
			Noted for good work, coolness + efficiency on night 1st/2nd - Corpl. Preston + 2/Lt/Cpl. Thomson. Others noted for good work + coolness during wiring operations + not mentioned in daily reports - 2 Cpl. Steadman, Sapper Kingston, Driver Harvey.	
	2ND TO 7TH		Completed doubling GINCHY Duckwalk Loop. Constructed BULL Dump Duckwalk Loop. Completed improvements GUILLEMONT Camp - Remade bunks in 3 shelters, floored remaining 33 shelters. New cookhouse	

1577 Wt. W10791/1773 500,000 1/15 D. D. & L. A.D.S.S./Forms/C. 2118.

CONTINUED TO PAGE 2

Instructions regarding War Diaries and Intelligence Summaries are contained in F. S. Regs., Part II. and the Staff Manual respectively. Title pages will be prepared in manuscript.

Army Form C. 2118.

WAR DIARY of 510TH (LONDON) FIELD COY. R.E. ~~or~~ ~~INTELLIGENCE SUMMARY.~~ FOR MONTH OF FEBRUARY 1917.

(*Erase heading not required.*)

Place	Date	Hour	Summary of Events and Information	Remarks and references to Appendices
B.E.F.			for Officers. New cookhouse for men. New latrine for Officers, ditto. for sergeants, two ditto for men.	
	5TH		II Lieut. Harden with advance party to MORLANCOURT + GROVE TOWN.	
	7TH		No. 2 Section to MEAULTE.	
			No. 4 Section to 9th Squadron R.F.C. - K.10.a. - near MORLANCOURT.	
	8TH		Headquarters joined No. 4 Section.	
			No. 1 + 3 Sections + Mounted Section to GROVE TOWN.	
			Hearty congratulations from the Corps Commander to Pioneers + R.Es on their consolidation in N.36. shown by air reports to be better than he imagined. XIV Corps G 142/3 of 3-2-17	
	8TH to 18TH		Work in Rest Area.	
			No. 2 Section - Baths at MEAULTE. Completing new baths + shifting engine + boiler etc.	
			No. 4 " - 9TH Sq. R.F.C. Aerodrome near MORLANCOURT. erecting Hangars	
			No. 1+3 " XIV Corps Rest Station. GROVE TOWN. erecting hutting	
	18TH		Company to WEDGE WOOD B.1.d.8.2. - less	
			No. 2 Section - remaining at MEAULTE ~~to complete~~ work on Baths.	
			No. 4 " to BRONFAY FARM for work on Camp, II Lieut Harden being appointed D.O.R.E.	
	19TH to 24TH		The two sections + H.Q. at WEDGE WOOD. B.1.d.8.2. employed on erecting Nissen huts ✗; latrines + cookhouses at HARDECOURT Camp (an infantry staging camp for 2 battalions)	
	25TH		No. 2 Section from MEAULTE rejoined Company at WEDGE WOOD.	
	25TH to 28TH		Three Sections + H.Q. employed as stated for 19TH to 25TH	
			✗ Less 25 Sprs at C.R.E.'s Workshop + 13 Sprs employed by him at dumps.	

1577 Wt. W10791/1773 500,000 1/15 D. D. & L. A.D.S.S./Forms/C. 2118.

CONTINUED TO PAGE 3

Instructions regarding War Diaries and Intelligence Summaries are contained in F. S. Regs., Part II. and the Staff Manual respectively. Title pages will be prepared in manuscript.

WAR DIARY OF 510TH (LONDON) FIELD COY. R.E.

or ~~INTELLIGENCE SUMMARY.~~ FOR MONTH OF FEBRUARY 1917.

(Erase heading not required.)

Army Form C. 2118.

Place	Date	Hour	Summary of Events and Information	Remarks and references to Appendices
			General.	
			On the 8th II Lieut. E.H. Wainwright left for five weeks course at Fourth Army Infantry School of Instruction.	
			On the 23rd Major W. Macrae left for Course of Instruction for R.E. Officers at LE PARCQ.	
			On the 15th the N.C.Os + men of the Coy received new numbers in the general R.E: Roll.	
			Honours received during the month.	
			No 548140 Sergt. HIGGS. E.H. awarded Military Medal for gallant conduct on Jan. 27th/28th. Auth: 29th Divl. R.O. 642 d/5-2-17.	
			No 548262 Sergt. HOLT. P. awarded D.C.M. for gallant conduct during operations of the 27th/28th Jan. 1917. Auth: 29th Divl. R.O. 647 d/12-2-17	
			B.J. Ryan Capt. R.E. for O.C. 510th (London) Fld. Coy. R.E. 28/2/17.	

1577 Wt. W10791/1773 500,000 1/15 D. D. & L. A.D.S.S./Forms/C. 2118.

Vol 9

CONFIDENTIAL.

W A R D I A R Y

O F

510th (London) Field Co.,R.E.

From 1st March, 1917 To 31st March, 1917

(V O L U M E I)

WAR DIARY of 510th (LONDON) FIELD COY. R.E. ~~or INTELLIGENCE SUMMARY.~~ FOR MONTH OF MARCH 1917

Army Form C. 2118.

Instructions regarding War Diaries and Intelligence Summaries are contained in F. S. Regs., Part II. and the Staff Manual respectively. Title pages will be prepared in manuscript.

(Erase heading not required.)

Place	Date	Hour	Summary of Events and Information	Remarks and references to Appendices
B. E. F.			Location of Company. Three Sections + H.Qrs. at WEDGE WOOD. B.1.d.8.2.	
			No 4 Section complete at BRONFAY FARM.	
			The following details worked directly under C.R.E. – 25 Sappers at C.R.E's workshop – 13 Sappers employed by him on dumps.	
	1st to 2nd		The three Sections at WEDGE WOOD were employed on erecting a NISSEN hut Camp at HARDECOURT.	
			No 4 Section at BRONFAY worked on hut erection + repairs under its officer who was D.O.R.E. for the Camp + also had 170 infantry (tradesmen) under him. The infantry were called the Divisional Hutting Coy.	
	3rd		Company to TREUX to Billets.	
			The Hutting Company remained attached to Coy. + moved with it into billets.	
			Mounted Portion moved by road, dismounted by rail from the PLATEAU to BUIRE.	
	4th to 11th		Overhauling equipment, painting vehicles + training. Physical drill in mornings with squad + Coy drill after breakfast.	
	8th		Hutting Company Disbanded, a few men remaining for work on Laundry, attached to this Company pending transfer to it.	
	12th		Major MACRAE returned from Course of Instruction.	
			C.R.E. inspected Coy. with the other two Coys. of Divisional Engineers.	
	13th		Inspection by G.O.C. Division – including bridging by the Company.	
	14th to 17th		Continued training – including route march, wiring + intensive digging.	

1577 Wt. W10791/1773 500,000 1/15 D. D. & L. A.D.S.S./Forms/C. 2118.

CONTINUED TO PAGE 2.

Instructions regarding War Diaries and Intelligence Summaries are contained in F. S. Regs., Part II. and the Staff Manual respectively. Title pages will be prepared in manuscript.

WAR DIARY of 510th (LONDON) FIELD COY. R.E. ~~or INTELLIGENCE SUMMARY.~~ FOR MONTH OF MARCH 1917.

(Erase heading not required.)

Army Form C. 2118.

Place	Date	Hour	Summary of Events and Information	Remarks and references to Appendices
B. E. F.	18th		Advanced party to SAISSEVAL & SAISSEMONT.	
			Transport to DAOURS joining 88th Brigade Transport there.	
	19th		Transport to ARGOEUVES.	
			Company by road to EDGE HILL Station.	
			" " train " HANGEST.	
			" " road " SAISSEVAL & SAISSEMONT.	
	20th		Transport joined the Company.	
	21st–29th		Training.	
	30th		Company, affiliated to 88th Brigade, marched by road to FLESSELLES.	
	31st		Halted at FLESSELLES.	
			Honours.	
			548262 Sergt HOLT. P. awarded D.C.M. } Gazette Auth: Supplement to London Gazette dated 12-3-17.	
			548140 " HIGGS. E. H. " M.M. }	
			548286 Sergt. EAST. O. J. " M.M. } Auth: Supplement to London Gazette dated 9-11-16.	
			548130 2/Cpl. GRAY. T. " " }	
			1669 Sapper CORNELL. L. " " }	
			1545 " GODWYN. J. " " }	
			548113 " MEDHURST. C. " " }	
			[signature] Major RE 31-3-17 O.C. 510 (London) Fd. Co. R.E.	

<u>C O N F I D E N T I A L.</u>

War Diary

of

510th (London) Field Co.,R.E.

From 1st April, 1917 To 30th April, 1917.

V O L U M E X.

-o-o-o-o-

Instructions regarding War Diaries and Intelligence Summaries are contained in F. S. Regs., Part II. and the Staff Manual respectively. Title pages will be prepared in manuscript.

WAR DIARY OF 510TH (LONDON) FIELD COY. R.E. or ~~INTELLIGENCE SUMMARY.~~ FOR MONTH OF APRIL 1917.

Army Form C. 2118.

(Erase heading not required.)

Place	Date	Hour	Summary of Events and Information	Remarks and references to Appendices
B.E.F.	1ST		Company marched from FLESSELLES to BEAUVAL.	
	2ND		" BEAUVAL to GRENAS. (LENS Map 1:100,000 - 5.F.4.9.	
	3RD		Dumped bridging equipment at MONDICOURT – Drew wood for boxing wagons, tools + stores.	
	4TH		Made boxes for the bridging wagons + drew more stores.	
	5TH		Company marched to IVERGNY - 4.E.7.8½.	
	6TH		Halted at IVERGNY.	
	7TH		Marched to COULLEMONT - 4.F.7.5½.	
	8TH + 9TH		Halted at COULLEMONT.	
	10TH		Marched to GOUY-EN-ARTOIS - P.18.d. - FRANCE Sheet 51C 1:40.000.	
	11TH		Halted in GOUY.	
	12TH		Breakfast at 5.45 a.m. + marched towards ARRAS. Halted for 2 hours outside ARRAS, + again halted for 3 hours in ARRAS. Marched out at 6.30 p.m. Arrived at midnight at FEUCHY CHAPEL Cross Roads - Bivouaced in Quarry at N.3.b.9.2½ (Taken over from 12th Div.)	
	13TH		Transport arrived about 1 a.m. + unloaded until 2.a.m. - Casualties to sappers - C.S.M. supervised evacuation of wounded successfully - L/Cpl. Strand doing well as Medical Orderly. Toolcarts left near bivouac. Animals + remaining transport left at 2.a.m for ARRAS. Moved Company less HQ to bivouac at H.33.d.2.2.	
	night 13/14		Work under Major B.T. WILSON. R.E. (W.R. Field Coy.) - Nos 3 + 4 Sections wired gap in wall - behind + overlapping gap - at MONCHY at O.1.b.0.3. - Sergt. HOLT wounded by grenade on way back - a loss to the Company.	
	night 14/15		Work under Major RUSTON (Kent Field Coy.) - Nos 1 + 2 Sections made Strong Point behind the above wire - in CHATEAU Garden, + infantry manned the Post. The 3 R.E. Companies thanked by G.O.C. for work on nights 13/14 + 14/15 in MONCHY-LE-PREUX. The drivers lead up 10 Pack Mules on this night with material + dumped near MONCHY.	

CONTINUED TO PAGE 2

Instructions regarding War Diaries and Intelligence Summaries are contained in F. S. Regs., Part II. and the Staff Manual respectively. Title pages will be prepared in manuscript.

WAR DIARY OF 510TH (LONDON) FIELD COY. R.E.

or

~~INTELLIGENCE SUMMARY.~~ FOR MONTH OF APRIL 1917.

(Erase heading not required.)

Army Form C. 2118.

Place	Date	Hour	Summary of Events and Information	Remarks and references to Appendices
B. E. F.	Night 15/16		Work under Major WILSON (W. RIDING Fld. Coy.) – All 4 sections wiring in front of front trench EAST of MONCHY-LE-PREUX from O.1.d.3.5. northwards. – Drivers took 14 mules into MONCHY under 2/Corpl. SNOW who did well – Nos 3 + 4 Sections caught by barrage at close of the work; the undermentioned showed up well A/Sergt. PRESTON, Corpl. WILLETT. 2/Cpl. WALKER, L/Cpl. ALLARD (Worcesters attchd. R.E.) + Sapper WARD. (reported by 2/Lieut. HARDEN.)	
	16th		Moved Company H.Q. to join Company in bivouac at H.33.d.2.2.	
	17th to 19th		Nos 1 + 2 Sections went to MONCHY-LE-PREUX, returning on 19th. Wiring done on 17th + 18th. Conditions were nasty + the following showed up well, besides the sergeants + corporals – 2/Cpl. HINWOOD, L/Cpls. RIX + WILLIAMS, Sappers CHANDLER, ARMSTRONG, POULTER + SMITH. A.G. – Corpl. GRAY. wounded – a heavy loss.	
	17/18 + 18/19		Mules again took material past front line to barricade EAST of MONCHY – 2/Cpl. WALKER acting as guide very satisfactorily – The work was well done under 2/Cpl. SNOW + then under L/Cpl. PERKINS.	
	19th		Capt. RYAN relieved Major MACRAE forward – In evening worked on trench board track, continuing work of W. RIDING Field Coy.	
	20th		Moved Coy. H.Q., 2 Sections + Mules back to H.32.d.3.9. – Completed trench board track.	
	21st		Brought 90 men back to bathe in ARRAS. Moved rear billets to RUE DU TEMPLE.	
	22nd		Maintained the duckboard + completed section bivouacs. Major MACRAE relieved Capt. RYAN forward – No. of Pack Mules made up to 20.	
	23/24		Went wiring with 50 MIDDLESEX + 50 L.F. after second attack. No 3 Section wired in front of SHRAPNEL TRENCH O.8.a.0.7. – The Middlesex party broken by H.E. + remainder lost touch – only a little material arriving. Sapper WARD showed up well, also L/Cpl. CLARKE. 2/Cpl. HINWOOD did well preparing material at dump until I ordered him to stop work owing to heavy fire	

CONTINUED TO PAGE 3.

Instructions regarding War Diaries and Intelligence Summaries are contained in F. S. Regs., Part II. and the Staff Manual respectively. Title pages will be prepared in manuscript.

WAR DIARY of 510TH (LONDON) FIELD COY. R.E.

Army Form C. 2118.

or

~~INTELLIGENCE SUMMARY.~~ FOR MONTH OF APRIL 1917.

(Erase heading not required.)

Place	Date	Hour	Summary of Events and Information	Remarks and references to Appendices
B.E.F.	24TH		Company moved back to MONTENESCOURT - 3.H.5.5. (LENS Map 1:100,000) Transport arrived after midnight - 56TH Field Coy. relieved this Coy.	
	25TH		Kit inspection, baths + re-loaded vehicles.	
	26TH		Marched to GOUY-EN-ARTOIS. 4.H.1.9½. - LENS Map 1:100,000.	
	27TH		Marched to SAILLY-AU-BOIS 5.H.1½.4½. - LENS Map 1:100,000. A new experience to arrive in a village, once full of troops, but now empty except for a small salvage section + a few inhabitants returned during the last week. This experience opens ones eyes to the enormous amount of material left behind for salvage in + round a village hurriedly vacated by a brigade + by heavy artillery on their moving forward.	
	28-30		Halted at SAILLY-AU-BOIS - resting, re-fitting + training.	

General notes.

Effective Strength of Unit		Officers.	O.R.
A.F.B. 213 of 31-3-17	-	5	199
" " " 28-4-17	-	6	201

Casualties during above period:-

Killed - 4 O.R.
Died of Wounds - 3 O.R.
Wounded - 7 "
Wounded slightly at duty - 5 O.R.
Evacuated sick - 3 O.R.
Transferred - 1 "

. Reinforcements - 1 officer + 20 O.R (including 15 infantry transferred to R.E. after being attached from battalions of the 88th Brigade to the Company pending transfer.)

[signature] Major RE 30-4-17
O.C. 510 (London) Fd. Co. RE

C O N F I D E N T I A L .

War Diary

of

510th (LONDON) FIELD COMPANY R. E.

From 1st of May 1917 to 31st May 1917

VOLUME I PART II

-p-o-o-o-o-o-o

Vol XI

Army Form C. 2118.

WAR DIARY of 510th (LONDON) FIELD COY. R.E.

~~or~~

~~INTELLIGENCE SUMMARY.~~ FOR MONTH OF MAY 1917.

(Erase heading not required.)

Instructions regarding War Diaries and Intelligence Summaries are contained in F. S. Regs., Part II. and the Staff Manual respectively. Title pages will be prepared in manuscript.

Place	Date	Hour	Summary of Events and Information	Remarks and references to Appendices
B. E. F.	1st		Marched from SAILLY-AU-BOIS - 5.H.1½.4½. LENS Map 1:100.000 to ST AMAND - 5.G.7.9 LENS Map 1:100.000.	
	2nd		Company moved to CASERNE LÉVIS, ARRAS - Transport by road, dismounted by road & tactical train, & on arrival ceased to be under orders of 88th Brigade.	
	3rd to 6th		Halted. Made B.W. Concertinas, latrine boxes &c.	
	7th		Marched to DAINVILLE - 3.I.6½.3½. - LENS Map 1:100.000.	
	8th to 12th		Halted. Training & Work in DAINVILLE & BERNEVILLE. Parties also sent out to tape strong posts in support line.	
	13th		Marched to ARRAS.	
			Night 13/14 - Party under Capt RYAN taped alignment for wiring support line.	
	14th to 15th		At ARRAS - Workshops & dumps.	
			Advance party took over camp of 438 (Cheshire) Fld. Co. R.E. on 14th but returned on 15th.	
			8 Sappers lent to 4th WORCESTER Regt. by order.	
	16th		Moved to bivouac H.25.b.4.3. & took over from 87th Fld. Coy R.E., also all dumps &c of 12th Divn.	
			Transport WEST of ARRAS. Workshop party in ARRAS.	
	17th to 23rd		Took over work on two Battn. H.Q. mined dug-outs, work left by 179 Tunnelling Coy. R.E., one dug-out in BAYONET TRENCH, the other in RIFLE TRENCH. Work in 3 shifts. 8 a.m. to 2 p.m., 2 p.m. to 8 a.m. 9.30 p.m. to 3.30 a.m. - Also working FEUCHY Rail-head Dump, IVORY Dump, IVORY workshops, & Saw mill, RUE DE MOULINET, ARRAS.	
	21st		Moved Transport lines & rear Coy. H.Q. to G.29.a.2.9.	
	22nd		Moved forward billet to H.20.a.5.4.	
	23rd		Handed over BAYONET TRENCH dug-out work to the New Zealand Engineers Tunnelling Coy.	
	24th		In addition to other work, sent 8 sappers to work with infantry on mined dug-outs in 4 strong posts; 11 Lieut. HARDEN taped a trench for infantry to dig.	

1577 Wt. W10791/1773 500,000 1/15 D. D. & L. A.D.S.S./Forms/C. 2118.

CONTINUED TO PAGE 2

Instructions regarding War Diaries and Intelligence Summaries are contained in F. S. Regs., Part II. and the Staff Manual respectively. Title pages will be prepared in manuscript.

WAR DIARY OF 510TH (LONDON) FIELD COY. R.E.

~~or~~

~~INTELLIGENCE SUMMARY.~~ FOR MONTH OF MAY 1917.

(*Erase heading not required.*)

Army Form C. 2118.

Place	Date	Hour	Summary of Events and Information	Remarks and references to Appendices
B.E.F.	25TH TO 31ST		Continued work on RIFLE TRENCH mined dug-out, 8 men still in the strong posts with the infantry - 2 per post. Spare men making Barbed Wire Concertinas, & when Infantry have carried up sufficient material; 2 extra men sent for night work on the Infantry Strong Posts.	

General Notes:-

Effective strength of Unit - Officers - Other Ranks

	Officers	Other Ranks
A.F.B. 213 of 28-4-17	7	201
A.F.B. 213 of 26-5-17	7	215

(Includes 1 officer posted, but temporarily attached to 497 (KENT) Field Coy. R.E.)

Casualties during above period. Other Ranks.

	Other Ranks
Killed	1
Wounded	2
Wounded slightly, at duty.	4
Evacuated sick	13
Posted to other Unit	1
Reinforcements	31

B. J. Ryan Capt. R.E.
for O.C. 510th (London) Fld Coy R.E.

1577 Wt. W10791/1773 500,000 1/15 D. D. & L. A.D.S.S./Forms/C. 2118.

Vol 12

CONFIDENTIAL.

War Diary

of

510th (London) Field Co.,R.E.

From 1st June, 1917. To 30th June, 1917.

VOLUME XII.

Instructions regarding War Diaries and Intelligence Summaries are contained in F. S. Regs., Part II. and the Staff Manual respectively. Title pages will be prepared in manuscript.

WAR DIARY of 510th (LONDON) FIELD COY. R.E.

~~or~~

~~INTELLIGENCE SUMMARY.~~ for MONTH OF JUNE 1917.

(Erase heading not required.)

Army Form C. 2118.

Place	Date	Hour	Summary of Events and Information	Remarks and references to Appendices
B.E.F.	1st		Forward Camp in tents at H.20.a.5.4. SCARPE VALLEY. – Transport & Rear H.Q. at G.29.a.2.9., 37, rue de DOUAI, ARRAS. – Work :- FEUCHY RY. DUMP, IVORY DUMP, IVORY Workshops & SAW MILL, 6 rue de MOULINET, ARRAS.	
			Continued work on mined DUG-OUT, RIFLE TRENCH I.3.a.3.4. – Exclusive of Steps – 550 sq. ft. done, about 120 sq. ft. remaining, after last shift on night 1st/2nd.	
			Continued work with 2 Sappers for Mined Dug-outs in each of 4 Strong Posts.	
	2nd		Forward Camp relieved by 56th Fld. Coy. R.E.; & moved back to Rear Head Quarters.	
	3rd		Sent on Advanced party. Dumps & Workshops handed over to 3rd Division.	
			Transport moved to BERNEVILLE (with 88th Bde. Transport.)	
	4th		Transport to LUCHEUX, picking up pontoons at MONDICOURT.	
			Personnel by rail from ARRAS to CANDAS & by road to CANAPLES.	
	5th		Transport from LUCHEUX to CANAPLES.	
	5th to 17th		At CANAPLES – Resting, re-fitting, work for the Brigade (88th), mostly in connection with baths & water supply, & training.	
	18th		Coy. marched to CANDAS to entrain & moved by train to PROVEN.	
	19th		Arrived PROVEN at 7 a.m. & marched to bivouac near ST. SIXTE. – Transport & H.Q. & 1 Section remained at this bivouac; the other 3 sapper sections moved by rail to just WEST of ELVERDINGHE & went into bivouac, with 300 Artillery detailed by XIV Corps for work on Artillery O.Ps. – 26 O.Ps. – of all descriptions including reinforced concrete.	
	20th		Officers & N.C.Os. shewn sites of O.Ps. – Carrying parties took materials to the O.P. sites after dark.	
	21st		Work commenced on 9 different O.Ps.	
	22nd to 30th		Work continued on O.Ps. 12 now in progress. – During this period it became necessary owing to shelling of bivouac to move it twice.	

1577 Wt. W10791/1773 500,000 1/15 D. D. & L. A.D.S.S./Forms/C. 2118.

CONTINUED TO PAGE 2.

Instructions regarding War Diaries and Intelligence Summaries are contained in F. S. Regs., Part II. and the Staff Manual respectively. Title pages will be prepared in manuscript.

WAR DIARY OF 510TH (LONDON) FIELD COY. R.E

~~or~~

~~INTELLIGENCE SUMMARY.~~ FOR MONTH OF JUNE 1917

(*Erase heading not required.*)

Army Form C. 2118.

Place	Date	Hour	Summary of Events and Information	Remarks and references to Appendices
			General Notes:-	
			Effective Strength of Unit - Officers - Other ranks.	
			A.F.B. 213 of 26-5-17 — 7 — 215	
			A.F.B. 213 of 30-6-17 — 7 — 207	
			(Includes 1 officer posted but temporarily attached to 497 (Kent) Field Coy. R.E.)	
			Casualties during above period - Other ranks.	
			Killed — 1	
			Wounded — 6	
			Wounded slightly, at duty — 2	
			Evacuated sick — 12	
			Reinforcements — 11	
			Honours received during the month:-	
			ii Lieut. G.B. HARDEN. - MILITARY CROSS - Auth: Birthday Honours 1917.	
			Major W. MACRAE. - Mentioned in Despatches - Auth: London Gazette 15th May, list in connection with despatches of 9th April 17.	
			W Macrae Major RE 30-6-17	

1577 Wt. W10791/1773 500,000 1/15 D. D. & L. A.D.S.S./Forms/C. 2118.

No 13

C O N F I D E N T I A L.

War Diary

of

510th (London) Field Company R.E.

From 1st July, 1917 to 30th July, 1917.

VOLUME XIII.

-*-*-

Army Form C. 2118.

Instructions regarding War Diaries and Intelligence Summaries are contained in F. S. Regs., Part II. and the Staff Manual respectively. Title pages will be prepared in manuscript.

WAR DIARY OF 510TH (LONDON) FIELD COY. R.E. ~~or INTELLIGENCE SUMMARY.~~ FOR MONTH OF JULY 1917.

(Erase heading not required.)

Place	Date	Hour	Summary of Events and Information	Remarks and references to Appendices
B. E. F.	1st to 13th		Major W. MACRAE. R.E. left to report to W.O. for further orders for India.	
			Company in Bivouac between ELVERDINGHE and WOESTEN with H.Q section and Drivers under 2 Lieut. ADAMS at INTERNATIONAL CORNER. Work in progress on O.Ps. for XIV CORPS. 6 R.A. Officers and 300 men (nominally) attached to and living with the Company in the same camp. These were employed on carrying + loading + unloading materials and for unskilled work on O.Ps. One R.A. Officer acted as Camp Commandant and produced the working parties as asked for for the work in progress. 18 O.Ps. of all descriptions in course of construction. Handcarts and trench tramway trucks employed to get forward materials from dumps in ELVERDINGE and on the CANAL BANK. It was found that the congestion of traffic on the roads at night made it not worth while to use G.S. Wagons to take materials from these dumps any further forward.	
	11th		Company ~~specially~~ complimented by Corps Commander on excellent work done in conjunction with R.A. working parties on construction of O.Ps.	
	14th		O.Ps. finished, 26 in all.	
			Sappers employed on small improvements to them. R.A. Officers and O.Rs. returned to their Batteries and D.A.Cs.	
	15th		The whole Company returned to the Company Horse Lines at INTERNATIONAL CORNER.	
	16th		Company resting + bathing less 8 Carpenters employed at C.R.E's workshops.	

1577 Wt. W10791/1773 500,000 1/15 D. D. & L. A.D.S.S./Forms/C. 2118.

CONTINUED TO PAGE 2.

Instructions regarding War Diaries and Intelligence Summaries are contained in F. S. Regs., Part II. and the Staff Manual respectively. Title pages will be prepared in manuscript.

WAR DIARY OF 510TH (LONDON) FIELD COY. R.E.

~~or~~

~~INTELLIGENCE SUMMARY.~~ FOR MONTH OF JULY 1917.

(Erase heading not required.)

Army Form C. 2118.

Place	Date	Hour	Summary of Events and Information	Remarks and references to Appendices
B.E.F.	17th		31 O.Rs. left to work on construction of Hospital Huts for XIV Corps under C.R.E. XIV Corps. Rationed & living with 4th C.C.S.	
	18th		Company resting and preparing site of new Camp.	
	19th		Moved to new Camp at A.10.b.6.4. in the wood.	
	19th to 26th		Two Sections employed at 4th C.C.S. on hutting for Hospital.	
			Remainder in camp at A.10.b.6.4. making camp and horse standings and overhauling equipment of Company and personnel. 12 O.R. at the sea-side for rest and sea-bathing under Corps arrangement.	
	27th		3 Officers & 100 O.R. arrived from Inf. Battalions of 88th Brigade to be attached permanently as carrying party & for unskilled work with Company.	
	28th to 30th		Training.	
	31st		The Coy. with 100 attached infantry less H.Q. & 10%, working on 2nd relief with 1 Batt. Infantry & 2 Coys. Pioneers on the road from BOESINGHE to C.1.a.25.15. & thence to CACTUS JUNCTION C.7.b.05.55. Hostile shell fire interfered with the work during this relief, the total casualties amounting to over 40. A good road for horse traffic was however made. Where the pavé was intact it was good enough even in the very wet weather, elsewhere (about 60% of the total length) corduroy would have to be laid for use in wet weather.	

1577 Wt. W10791/1773 500,000 1/15 D. D. & L. A.D.S.S./Forms/C. 2118.

CONTINUED TO PAGE 3.

WAR DIARY OF 510TH (LONDON) FIELD COY. R.E.

Army Form C. 2118.

~~or~~

~~INTELLIGENCE SUMMARY.~~ FOR MONTH OF JULY 1917.

(*Erase heading not required.*)

Instructions regarding War Diaries and Intelligence Summaries are contained in F. S. Regs., Part II. and the Staff Manual respectively. Title pages will be prepared in manuscript.

Place	Date	Hour	Summary of Events and Information	Remarks and references to Appendices
			General Notes :-	
			Effective Strength of Unit - Officers - Other Ranks.	
			A.F.B. 213 of 30-6-17 — 7x — 207	
			" " 28-7-17 — 8 — 215	
			x Includes 1 Officer posted but temporarily attached to 497 (Kent) Field Coy. R.E.	
			Casualties during above period - Officers - Other ranks.	
			Wounded — - — 1	
			Wounded slightly at duty — - — 6	
			Evacuated Sick — - — 5	
			Transferred to other Units — 2 — 1	
			Reinforcements — 3 — 15	
			Honours received during the month:-	
			548637 Sapper BEGLEY. J. } Awarded MILITARY MEDAL Auth: XIV Corps R.O. 566 d/27-7-17.	
			548323 " KINGSTON. W. }	
			B. J. Ryan CAPT. R.E.	
			O.C. 510TH (LONDON) FIELD COY. R.E.	

1577 Wt. W10791/1773 500,000 1/15 D. D. & L. A.D.S.S./Forms/C. 2118.

CONFIDENTIAL.

War Diary

of

510th (London) Field Company R.E.

From 1st August, 1917 to 31st August, 1917.

VOLUME XIV.

-*-*-

Instructions regarding War Diaries and Intelligence Summaries are contained in F. S. Regs., Part II. and the Staff Manual respectively. Title pages will be prepared in manuscript.

WAR DIARY OF 510TH (LONDON) FIELD COY. R.E. ~~or INTELLIGENCE SUMMARY.~~ FOR MONTH OF AUGUST 1917.

Army Form C. 2118.

(Erase heading not required.)

Place	Date	Hour	Summary of Events and Information	Remarks and references to Appendices
B.E.F.	1		Location of the Coy. BELGIUM sheet 28 N.W. scale 1:20.000. Coy in tents + shelters in the wood at A.10.b.6.4.	
			Work continued on clearing earth off pavé road forward from BOESINGHE to C.1.a.3.2.	
	2		10 A.S.C. G.S. waggons attached to Coy + 2 Coy bridging waggons used to carry forward beech planks to the above road for corduroying it.	
	3		Worked with 60 of attached Infantry on laying corduroy from C.1.a.3.2. towards C.1.c.7.3. Forty sappers. 76 yards done in 6 hours. Materials carried 300 yards.	
	4		Waggons carting beech planking as on 2nd.	
	5		Laid corduroy. Thirty sappers + carrying party of about 120 Infantry working in three places. A total of 48 yards was done in four hours. Half of the material on site, half carried about 800 yards.	
	6		Coy came back onto work for 29th Division. Made rough shelter for tea shop on EAST bank of CANAL at BOESINGHE. Made a foot washing bath at ELVERDINGHE both completed roughly ready for use.	
	7		Continued work on baths at ELVERDINGHE. Took over dump at ONDANK for C.R.E.	

CONTINUED TO PAGE 2.

Instructions regarding War Diaries and Intelligence Summaries are contained in F. S. Regs., Part II. and the Staff Manual respectively. Title pages will be prepared in manuscript.

WAR DIARY of 510TH (LONDON) FIELD COY. R.E.
or
INTELLIGENCE SUMMARY. FOR MONTH OF AUGUST 1917.
(Erase heading not required.)

Army Form C. 2118.

Place	Date	Hour	Summary of Events and Information	Remarks and references to Appendices
B.E.F.			+ part 80 sappers + 80 attached Infantry on making duck boards.	
	8		Loading lorries + unloading. Making duck boards at dump. Finishing off baths.	
	9 TO 13		Dump + workshop preparations for attack. Making light bridges + trestles for infantry crossings over STEENBEEK. Artillery bridges, notice boards, mats for crossing marshes.	
	14		Moved whole Coy. into camp at LUNAVILLE FARM. S.W. of BOESINGHE.	
	15-16		Making two strong points on outskirts of LANGEMARCK (night work.)	
	16		Commenced trench tramway from PILCKEM RIDGE to STEENBEEK. Work on laying mats across marsh behind our front line.	
	17		Continued above work + started screening in forward area.	
	25		As above. Trench tramway finished including portion up to WIJDENDRIFT ROAD.	
	26		Coy moved to PROVEN area. Dismounted personnel by rail, mounted by road. Took over camp of 76TH Field Coy. R.E. in P.2. area Sheet 19 S.E. X.28.a.3.9. S. of CROMBEKE on CROMBEKE - POPERINGHE road. Barn for drivers. Bivouac sheets for sappers. No latrines or construction at all. "Lieut G.L. SYMONS evacuated sick.	
	27		Coy. employed on improvement of bivouacs. No material. Heavy rain. Major B.J. RYAN went on leave	

continued to page 3

Instructions regarding War Diaries and Intelligence Summaries are contained in F. S. Regs., Part II. and the Staff Manual respectively. Title pages will be prepared in manuscript.

WAR DIARY OF 510TH (LONDON) FIELD COY R.E.
or
INTELLIGENCE SUMMARY.
(Erase heading not required.)

Army Form C. 2118.

Place	Date	Hour	Summary of Events and Information	Remarks and references to Appendices
B.E.F.	28		Training & kit inspections. One section on work in camp, latrines, cookhouses &c.	
	29		Work on cinema hut PROVEN & 88th Bde. Camps. Training.	
	30-31		ditto. ditto.	
	30		" Lieut. H.V. SHOVE joined Coy. from Base.	

General Notes:

	Officers	O.R.
Effective Strength of Unit - AFB. 213 of 28-7-17	8	215
" " " 25-8-17	5	203
Casualties during above period:	-	
Killed	-	2
Died of wounds	-	1
Wounded	1	10
" slightly at duty	-	4
Evacuated sick	-	2
Transferred	2	3
Reinforcements		6

Honours received during month:

207277 L/Cpl. PICKLES J.W. awarded M.M. Auth. XIV Corps R.O. 669 d/26-8-17.

[illegible]
Lieut. R.E.
for O.C. 510th (London) Field Coy. R.E.

C O N F I D E N T I A L.

War Diary

of

510th (London) Field Company R.E.

From 1st September, 1917, to 30th September, 1917.

VOLUME XV.

-*-*-*-

Vol 15

Instructions regarding War Diaries and Intelligence Summaries are contained in F. S. Regs., Part II. and the Staff Manual respectively. Title pages will be prepared in manuscript.

WAR DIARY OF 510TH (LONDON) FIELD COY. R.E.
or
~~INTELLIGENCE SUMMARY.~~ FOR MONTH OF SEPTEMBER 1917.

(Erase heading not required.)

Army Form C. 2118.

Place	Date	Hour	Summary of Events and Information	Remarks and references to Appendices
B. E. F.		1	Company located under canvas at CROMBEKE P2 Area. Training in drill & lectures	
		2	Church Parade.	
		3	Practice ceremonial parade.	
		4	Brigade rehersal of Divl. Parade for presentation of medal ribbons.	
		5	Brigade Parade Corpl. PICKLES J.W. of the Coy. received M.M. ribbon.	
		6	Training & intensive digging, wiring &c.	
		7	Coy moved to WHITE HOPE CORNER & took over work on roads from 83rd Fld. Coy. R.E. under C.E. XIV Corps. Road across PILKEM RIDGE to LANGEMARCK.	
			Transport & Coy H.Q. remained at CROMBEKE.	
		8	Roadwork. 1 Battn. of Infantry to assist.	
		9	" . Shelled out of camp & shifted to a quieter one at PARROY FARM.	
		10 to 13	Roadwork.	
		14	Relieved; the work being practically completed. Completion & maintenance taken over by a Tunnelling Coy R.E. Coy returned to camp at CROMBEKE.	
		15	Coy resting & cleaning up	

1577 Wt. W10791/1773 500,000 1/15 D. D. & L. A.D.S.S./Forms/C. 2118.

CONTINUED TO PAGE 2.

Instructions regarding War Diaries and Intelligence Summaries are contained in F. S. Regs., Part II. and the Staff Manual respectively. Title pages will be prepared in manuscript.

WAR DIARY of 510th (London) Field Coy R.E.
or
~~INTELLIGENCE SUMMARY.~~ for Month of September 1917

(Erase heading not required.)

Army Form C. 2118.

Place	Date	Hour	Summary of Events and Information	Remarks and references to Appendices
B.E.F.	16		Church Parade.	
	17		"Lieut. D.R. WILLIAMSON R.E. left Coy to be attached to H.Q. 29th Divl Engineers as Assistant Adjutant.	
			Coy bathing. Washing vehicles.	
	18		3 Officers + 100 O.R. Infantry reported from Battns. of 88th Brigade for attachment to Coy as Sapping Platoons during period that Coy is in the line.	
			Advance party took over maintenance of trench tramway from RUGBY Dump to WIJDENDRIFT ROAD + RUGBY R.E. Dump from Guards Divl R.E.	
	19		Company moved to ELVERDINGHE CHATEAU WALL DUGOUTS - Dismounted personnel by rail - Transport by road.	
			Transport lines near DE WIPPE CORNER.	
			Took over Divl R.E. dump at ONDANK. 1 NCO, 10 O.R. + 20 Infantry.	
	20		Work on repair of Canal Bridges. Pontoon, foot bridges + approaches.	
	21		Loading huts on lorries + erecting in Divl area. Lt R.W.O. HARTRIDGE, R.E. (T.F.) joined Coy.	
	22		Loading huts on lorries + erecting in Divl area.	

1577 Wt. W10791/1773 500,000 1/15 D. D. & L. A.D.S.S./Forms/C. 2118.

Continued to page 3.

Instructions regarding War Diaries and Intelligence Summaries are contained in F. S. Regs., Part II. and the Staff Manual respectively. Title pages will be prepared in manuscript.

WAR DIARY of 510th (LONDON) FIELD COY. R.E. or ~~INTELLIGENCE SUMMARY.~~ FOR MONTH OF SEPTEMBER 1917

Army Form C. 2118.

(Erase heading not required.)

Place	Date	Hour	Summary of Events and Information	Remarks and references to Appendices
B.E.F.	22		Repairs to approaches of both pontoon bridges. Carrying materials from decauville railway to RUGBY Dump.	
			Lieut ROBERTS 1/2 MONMOUTH Pioneers attached to Coy for instruction in R.E. duties	
	23		Church Parade. Commenced work on baths ELVERDINGHE CHATEAU 1 Section.	
	24		Trench tramway - Commenced switch from near PINSON FARM to junction of BRIDGE ST. + WIJDENDRIFT Road.	
			Moved RUGBY dump from PILCKEM Ridge forward to ABRI WOOD - Baths as before. - Commenced work on repair of Infantry camps in Divl. area.	
			Hutting section formed from 88th Bde. 1 Officer + 60. O.R.	
	25		Works as above. - Also screening of FOURCHE FARM, VULCAN CROSSING + ridge.	
	26		Shelling stopped all forward area work. Had to double tramway maintenance gang. line repaired by 6 p.m.	
	27 to 29		Work continued.	
	30		Tramway again broken in a lot of places.	

1577 Wt. W10791/1773 500,000 1/15 D. D. & L. A.D.S.S./Forms/C. 2118.

CONTINUED TO PAGE 4

Instructions regarding War Diaries and Intelligence Summaries are contained in F. S. Regs., Part II. and the Staff Manual respectively. Title pages will be prepared in manuscript.

WAR DIARY OF 510TH (LONDON) FIELD COY. R.E. Army Form C. 2118.

or

INTELLIGENCE SUMMARY. FOR MONTH OF SEPTEMBER 1917.

(Erase heading not required.)

Place	Date	Hour	Summary of Events and Information	Remarks and references to Appendices
			General notes :.	
			Effective Strength of Unit - Officers - Other ranks.	
			A.F.B. 213 of 25-8-17 — 5 — 203	
			" " 29-9-17 — 7 — 200	
			Casualties during above period.	
			Killed — — 1	
			Died of wounds — — 3	
			Wounded — 1 — 4	
			Wounded slightly at duty — — 4	
			Transferred — — 3	
			Evacuated sick — 1 — 5	
			Reinforcements. — 4 — 11	
			Honours received during Month.	
			548149 Sergt PRETON J.T. awarded D.C.M. - Auth. London Gazette d/18-9-17.	
			B. J. Ryan MAJOR R.E.	
			O.C. 510TH (LONDON) FIELD COY. R.E.	

1577 Wt. W10791/1773 500,000 1/15 D. D. & L. A.D.S.S./Forms/C. 2118.

Vol 16

C O N F I D E N T I A L

War Diary

of

510th (London) Field Company R.E.

From 1st October, 1917, to 31st October, 1917.

VOLUME XVI.

-*-*-*-

Instructions regarding War Diaries and Intelligence Summaries are contained in F. S. Regs., Part II. and the Staff Manual respectively. Title pages will be prepared in manuscript.

WAR DIARY of 510TH (LONDON) FIELD COY. R.E. ~~or~~ ~~INTELLIGENCE SUMMARY.~~ FOR MONTH OF OCTOBER 1917.

(Erase heading not required.)

Army Form C. 2118.

Place	Date	Hour	Summary of Events and Information	Remarks and references to Appendices
B.E.F.	1		Coy located in dugouts at ELVERDINGHE with Transport at ONDANK near C.R.E.s dump. Coy had attached to + living with it 100 infantry O.R. + 3 officers from 88th Brigade. Work constructing trench tramway from MARTINS MILL to Rly. line near LANGEMARCK. Screening various dugouts + roads, also across crest to right of PILCKEM for gun flashes.	
	2		Forming battle dump at VULCAN CROSSING on the PILCKEM - STADEN Rly by G.S. waggons. Screening + tramway as above.	
	3		10 G.S. waggons as above forming dump	
	4		Right of our Division attacked just on left of the STADEN Rly. forming pivot for troops on right. No work done because of severe shelling of forward area.	
	5		Screening VULCAN CROSSING Bde. H.Q., making gas proof doors + sandbagging. Tramway as above.	
	6		As on 5th 10 G.S. waggons to VULCAN CROSSING battle dump. The journey of about four miles from CANAL crossing to dump half a mile behind LANGEMARCK took 5 hours, owing to congestion of road by ammunition columns guns &c.	

1577 Wt. W10791/1773 500,000 1/15 D. D. & L. A.D.S.S./Forms/C. 2118.

CONTINUED TO PAGE II

Instructions regarding War Diaries and Intelligence Summaries are contained in F. S. Regs., Part II. and the Staff Manual respectively. Title pages will be prepared in manuscript.

WAR DIARY OF 510TH (LONDON) FIELD COY. R.E.
~~or~~
~~INTELLIGENCE SUMMARY.~~ FOR MONTH OF OCTOBER 1917.

(Erase heading not required.)

Army Form C. 2118.

Place	Date	Hour	Summary of Events and Information	Remarks and references to Appendices
B.E.F.	7		Put up A.D.S. at HANLEY, two large elephant shelters. Continued working on screening + tramway.	
	8		Resting for work on the 9th.	
	9		88th + 86th Bdes. attacked across the BROEMBEEK astride the STADEN Rly.	
			Coy. paraded at 6 a.m., moved to rendez-vous near VULCAN CROSSING carrying tools, sandbags etc. Moved forward as soon as troops had gone on to 3rd objective + made a track for mules along the STADEN Rly from LANGEMARCK to the BROEMBEEK. Also laid some german duck boards, found on the Rly., along the forward tape towards BROEMBEEK.	
			Taped out a track to MARCHAL FARM. Made three bridges for foot traffic + one for mules across the BROEMBEEK.	
	10		Coy. resting + loading vehicles.	
	11		Coy moved to bivouacs at SALEM CAMP 1500x S.E. of CROMBEKE. Sappers by train from ELVERDINGHE to INTERNATIONAL CORNER. Transport independantly by road. The 100 attached infantry rejoined their Units.	

1577 Wt. W10791/1773 500,000 1/15 D. D. & L. A.D.S.S./Forms/C. 2118.

CONTINUED TO PAGE 3.

Army Form C. 2118.

Instructions regarding War Diaries and Intelligence Summaries are contained in F. S. Regs., Part II. and the Staff Manual respectively. Title pages will be prepared in manuscript.

WAR DIARY OF 510TH (LONDON) FIELD COY. R.E.

or

~~INTELLIGENCE SUMMARY.~~ FOR MONTH OF OCTOBER 1917.

(Erase heading not required.)

Place	Date	Hour	Summary of Events and Information	Remarks and references to Appendices
B.E.F.	12		Overhauling equipment. Very wet.	
	13		do do + building shelters in camp.	
			C.E. XIV Corps thanked R.E. Coys of Divn for their work whilst in YPRES area.	
	14		Church Parade. 1 Sect. pulling down Divl. Theatre at ONDANK.	
	15		G.O.C. XIV Corps called at camp + thanked Coy for work done with Division whilst in YPRES area.	
			Loading.	
	16		Entrained at PESELHOEK. Train due to leave 11·22 p.m., left at 5 a.m. 17TH.	
	17		Detrained at SAULTY at 3 p.m. Made tea for Coy at station. Marched to POMMIER to camp. 1 section to BIENVILLERS.	
	18		Standing by for orders to move.	
	19		Marched to billets + huts at LA HERLIÈRE.	
	20		Unloading, washing vehicles + repairing huts	
	21		Sunday. Resting	
	22		Commenced erection of Divisional Theatre also pulling down huts at LA BAZÈQUE Chateau to move to BASSEAUX Divl. Area.	

1577 Wt. W10791/1773 500,000 1/15 D. D. & L. A.D.S.S./Forms/C. 2118.

CONTINUED TO PAGE 4

Army Form C. 2118.

Instructions regarding War Diaries and Intelligence Summaries are contained in F. S. Regs., Part II. and the Staff Manual respectively. Title pages will be prepared in manuscript.

WAR DIARY of 510TH (LONDON) FIELD COY. R.E.
~~or~~
~~INTELLIGENCE SUMMARY.~~ FOR MONTH OF OCTOBER 1917.

(Erase heading not required.)

Place	Date	Hour	Summary of Events and Information	Remarks and references to Appendices
B.E.F.	23		Putting up Divisional Theatre. Pulling down LA BAZEQUE camp. 100 infantry attached for purpose.	
	24		Orders for move arrived. Loading.	
	25		Transport left 8.30 a.m. to march to BAPAUME. Sappers left 11.30 a.m. to march to ARRAS. 2 motor lorries for kits, extra blanket + cooks. Tea ready at ARRAS on arrival. Entrained 6 p.m. with 1/2 455 Fld. Coy. + 29TH H.Q. R.E., 497 Fld. Coy. joined where we changed. Arrived FINS 11.30 p.m. 2 cookers of tea + transport waiting for the 2 1/2 R.E. Coys. Marched to huts at HEUDECOURT	
	26		Reconnoitred for Coy. billets at GOUZEAUCOURT + saw part of work. Moved to elephant shelters at R.31.a. S.E. of last named village. 1 section + tool-carts in a house in the village.	
	27		Reconnoitred sites for erection of elephant shelters in banks + sunken roads. Took N.C.Os. round. Unloaded, after dark, decauville train load of shelters, timber &c.	
	28		Commenced excavations. Also unloaded a train as above.	
	29		Got 6 shelters erected, they are dug into banks + are large french elephants 18 ft. long, no protection or sandbagging done beyond the excavation. Coy transport used to carry stores from decauville track to sites.	

1577 Wt. W10791/1773 500,000 1/15 D. D. & L. A.D.S.S./Forms/C. 2118.

CONTINUED TO PAGE 5

WAR DIARY of 510TH (LONDON) FIELD COY. R.E. Army Form C. 2118.

~~or~~

~~**INTELLIGENCE SUMMARY.**~~ FOR MONTH OF OCTOBER 1917.

(Erase heading not required.)

Instructions regarding War Diaries and Intelligence Summaries are contained in F. S. Regs., Part II. and the Staff Manual respectively. Title pages will be prepared in manuscript.

Place	Date	Hour	Summary of Events and Information	Remarks and references to Appendices
B.E.F.	30		3 shelters erected. Unloading train.	
	31		4 shelters erected.	
			General notes:-	
			Effective Strength of Unit — Officers / Other ranks	
			AFB 213 of 29-9-17 — 7 / 200	
			" " " 27-10-17 — 7 / 202	
			Casualties during above period.	
			Evacuated sick — 2	
			Reinforcements — 4	
			Honours received during month:	
			548192 Lce Corpl. MATTHEWS. F. awarded M.M. Auth: XIV Corps. R.O 790 d/ 6-10-17	

B. J. Ryan Maj: R.E.
OC. 510th (London) Fld. Coy R.E.
1/11/17

Vol 17

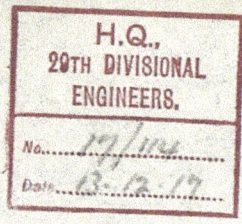

C O N F I D E N T I A L.

W A R D I A R Y.

OF

510TH. (LONDON) FIELD COY., R.E.,

VOLUME 17.

(November 1917)

CONFIDENTIAL.

WAR DIARY

OF

510TH (LONDON) FIELD COMPANY R.E.

VOLUME: 17.

Army Form C. 2118.

Instructions regarding War Diaries and Intelligence Summaries are contained in F. S. Regs., Part II. and the Staff Manual respectively. Title Pages will be prepared in manuscript.

WAR DIARY of 510th (LONDON) FIELD COY. R.E.
or
~~INTELLIGENCE SUMMARY~~ FOR MONTH OF NOVEMBER 1917

(Erase heading not required.)

Place	Date	Hour	Summary of Events and Information	Remarks and references to Appendices
B. E. F.	1		Coy situated at GOUZEAUCOURT. Transport at HEUDECOURT attached to 20th Division for rations, accomodation &c. Working under own C.R.E. on work for III Corps erecting dugouts in forward area. 497th + half 455th Field Coys working on the same job. Erected 4 elephant shelters.	
	1 - 14		Coy working in GOUZEAUCOURT on erecting elephant shelters. Transport at HEUDECOURT	
	15 - 20		Coy + transport moved to NURLU stopping one night at SOREL-LE-GRAND. Work in NURLU on erecting tarpaulin shelters. Shelters erected for 2 Battns.	
	20		Zero day One section with each Brigade. Transport to SOREL-LE-GRAND. Bridging wagons to TYKE dump. No 3 Section saved MARCOING bridge from demolition. Coy reassembled in HINDENBURG line.	
	21		Coy moved to MARCOING to construct bridge at NOYELLES	
	22		NOYELLES still in German hands.	
	28		Major RYAN + Corpl. HINWOOD reconnoitred bridges. Major RYAN wiped + evacuated. Coy moved to MASNIÈRES to work on MASNIÈRES defences. MASNIÈRES heavily shelled Casualties in billets. Work digging trenches, camouflage.	
	29 - 30		Coy moved back to GOUZEAUCOURT. German attack. Billets abandoned. Coy used in counter-attack. Most of Coy. equipment + officers + men's kits lost. Office burnt.	

2449 Wt. W14957/M90 750,000 1/16 J.B.C. & A. Forms/C.2118/12.

CONTINUED TO PAGE 11.

Army Form C. 2118.

Instructions regarding War Diaries and Intelligence Summaries are contained in F. S. Regs., Part II. and the Staff Manual respectively. Title Pages will be prepared in manuscript.

WAR DIARY OF 510TH (LONDON) FIELD COY. R.E.
or
~~INTELLIGENCE SUMMARY~~ FOR MONTH OF NOVEMBER.

(Erase heading not required.)

Place	Date	Hour	Summary of Events and Information	Remarks and references to Appendices
			General notes:	
			Effective strength of Unit — Officers / O.R.	
			A.F.B. 213 d/ 27-10-17 — 7 / 202	
			213 d/ 24-11-17 — 6 / 211	
			Casualties during above period: Officers / O.R.	
			Wounded — 1 / -	
			Transferred — 1 / -	
			Reinforcements — 1 / 9	
			30.12.17	
			[illegible signature] Capt RE OC 510th (London) Field Coy RE	

CONFIDENTIAL.

WAR DIARY

OF

510TH (LONDON) FIELD COY. R.E.

FROM DECEMBER 1ST TO DECEMBER 31ST 1917.

(VOLUME 18)

Army Form C. 2118.

Instructions regarding War Diaries and Intelligence Summaries are contained in F. S. Regs., Part II. and the Staff Manual respectively. Title pages will be prepared in manuscript.

WAR DIARY OF 510TH (LONDON) FIELD COY. R.E.
or
~~INTELLIGENCE SUMMARY.~~ FOR MONTH OF DECEMBER 1917

(Erase heading not required.)

Place	Date	Hour	Summary of Events and Information	Remarks and references to Appendices
B.E.F.	1		Coy resting at SOREL LE GRAND	
	2		" " "	
	3-4		Coy at RIBECOURT working with 88th Brigade on front line strongpoint against German attacks. Transport at SOREL-LE-GRAND.	
	4		Coy moved back to SOREL-LE-GRAND	
	5-6		Dismounted personnel entrained at ETRICOURT to MONDICOURT-PAS & marched to BERLENCOURT. Transport by road	
	7		Transport arrived at BERLENCOURT.	
	7-8		Cleaning up inspections of clothing equipment &c	
	9		Church parade 3 p.m.	
	10-13		Coy inspection parade in morning - ½-¾ hrs arm drill, physical drill &c. General cleaning up & small-kit inspections. Route march in afternoon	
	12		Section Transport accompanied Route march. D.A.D.V.S. visited lines in morning.	
	14		Coy inspection parade in morning. Coy had use of Baths for day & all men had a bath & clean change of underclothing. Physical drill, arm drill &c carried out at times depending on baths.	
	15		Coy inspection parade in morning ½-¾ hrs. arm drill, physical training &c.	
	16		C of E. Service in ECOLE at BERLENCOURT.	
	17		Coy inspection parade in morning. Cleaning road &c. Packing wagons.	
	18		Coy moved by road to AUBROMETZ.	

(A7092). Wt. W12839/M1293. 750,000. 1/17. D. D. & L., Ltd. Forms/C.2118/14.

CONTINUED TO PAGE 2.

Army Form C. 2118.

Instructions regarding War Diaries and Intelligence Summaries are contained in F. S. Regs., Part II. and the Staff Manual respectively. Title pages will be prepared in manuscript.

WAR DIARY OF 510TH (LONDON) FIELD COY. R.E.
or
~~INTELLIGENCE SUMMARY.~~ FOR MONTH OF DECEMBER 1917.

(Erase heading not required.)

Place	Date	Hour	Summary of Events and Information	Remarks and references to Appendices
B.E.F.	19		Coy. moved by road to BEALENCOURT. Half Transport had to remain at ROLLENCOURT owing to the roads being made almost impassable by snow.	
	20		Coy moved by road to ST. DENOEUX.	
	21		Resting.	
	22		Coy. inspection parade in morning. 1/2-3/4 hours arm drill, physical training &c. Parking & cleaning wagons.	
	23		Check parade & rifle inspection in morning. No Church Parade could be arranged.	
	24		Coy. inspection parade in morning. Physical training, arm drill &c.	
	25		Coy held a dinner at the ECOLE followed by a smoking concert.	
	26		No parades could be held owing to the weather. Section Officers lectured their Sections on Discipline, Saluting &c., Rapid Wiring both Single & Double Fence & Apron types. O.C. lectured officers on "Reports & Reconnaissances".	
	27		Coy inspection parade in morning. All Sections lectured on "Machine Guns" by Corpl. COLDMAN, 88th M.G. Coy. Arm drill, Physical training &c. Section Officers lectured their Sections on "Reports & Reconnaissances".	
	28		Coy. inspection parade in the morning. All sections lectured by their Officers on "Map Reading & the use of the Prismatic Compass" & also by Instructor from M.G.C. on the "Mechanism & method of firing a Vickers' M.G.". Physical training, Arm drill &c.	
	29		Coy inspection in the morning. Instruction in stoppages in Vickers' Gun. Description of Lewis Gun by Instructor from 88th Brigade. Gas drill, arm drill &c. 2 Sections instructed in practical work with Prismatic Compass & 2 Sections were lectured on "Map Reading".	

(A7092). Wt. W12839/M1293. 750,000. 1/17. D. D. & L., Ltd. Forms/C.2118/14.

CONTINUED TO PAGE 3.

Army Form C. 2118.

Instructions regarding War Diaries and Intelligence Summaries are contained in F. S. Regs., Part II. and the Staff Manual respectively. Title pages will be prepared in manuscript.

WAR DIARY of 510TH (LONDON) FIELD COY. R.E. ~~or INTELLIGENCE SUMMARY.~~ for MONTH OF DECEMBRE 1917

(Erase heading not required.)

Place	Date	Hour	Summary of Events and Information	Remarks and references to Appendices
B.E.F.	30		Check parade in morning. No Church Parade could be arranged.	
	31		Coy inspection parade in the morning. Instruction in Vickers + Lewis Guns. Arm drill + Physical training. 2 Sections instructed in Compass work + 2 Sections instructed in wiring.	

General notes December 1917.

Effective Strength of Unit	Officers	O.R.
A.F.B. 213 d/ 24-11-17	6	211
A.F.B. 213 d/ 29-12-17	8	187

Casualties during above period.

	Officers	O.R.
Died of Wounds		1
Wounded	1	11
Wounded slightly at duty		1
Missing		5
Evacuated		7
Transferred		4
Reinforcements	3	4

J. A. Parker.
MAJOR. R.E.
O.C. 510TH (London) Field Coy. R.E.

(A7092). Wt. W12839/M1293. 750,000. 1/17. D. D. & L., Ltd. Forms/C.2118/14.

7

Instructions regarding War Diaries and Intelligence Summaries are contained in F. S. Regs., Part II. and the Staff Manual respectively. Title pages will be prepared in manuscript.

WAR DIARY of 510th (LONDON) FIELD COY. R.E. ~~or INTELLIGENCE~~ SUMMARY. for MONTH of JANUARY 1918.

Army Form C. 2118.

(Erase heading not required.)

Vol 19

Place	Date	Hour	Summary of Events and Information	Remarks and references to Appendices
B.E.F.	1		at ST DENOEUX Coy training. All sections 1 hour Vickers M.G. Stoppages. 1 hour Lewis Gun. 2 sections practical reconnaissances 2 hours + 2 sections practised Divl. rapid wiring 2 hours. Part time arm drill &c as usual.	
			Work on bath house LEBIEZ started.	
			Orders received that Divn. less 87th Bde + D.A. would move to FRUGES area by march route on 3rd + 4th insts.	
	2		Training nil. Coy employed on loading + packing wagons + preparing for move.	
	3		Coy proceeded to HAPPE (near CAMPAGNE-LES-BOULONNAIS) by march route, via ST MICHEL, LEDINGHAM, QUILEN, MANINGHEM, WICQUINGHEM, CAMPAGNE. Distance 15 miles. Starting time 8.45. Coy (less transport) arrived HAPPE 16.30. Transport arrived HAPPE 23.00. Very tiring march for men + horses owing to state of roads, many of which were 6" deep in snow + to number of hills which lay on the route.	
	4		Coy moved from HAPPE to QUERCAMPS via THIEMBRONNE, WISMES, ELNES, ACQUIN. Distance 14 miles. Starting time 9.40. Coy less transport arrived QUERCAMPS 16.15. Transport arrived QUERCAMPS 19.00. Transport had to follow behind Coy owing to state of roads + number of hills.	

(A7092). Wt. W12839/M1293. 750,000. 1/17. D. D. & L., Ltd. Forms/C.2118/14.

CONTINUED TO PAGE 2.

Army Form C. 2118.

Instructions regarding War Diaries and Intelligence Summaries are contained in F. S. Regs., Part II. and the Staff Manual respectively. Title pages will be prepared in manuscript.

WAR DIARY OF 510TH (LONDON) FIELD COY. R.E.

~~or~~

~~**INTELLIGENCE SUMMARY.**~~ FOR MONTH OF JANUARY 1918.

(Erase heading not required.)

Place	Date	Hour	Summary of Events and Information	Remarks and references to Appendices
B.E.F.	4		Orders received at 21.45 that Coy would move on 5th inst to ST. MARTIN-AU-LAERT, & on 6th inst to forward area	
	5		Coy marched from QUERCAMP to ST MARTIN-AU-LAERT, via BOISDINGHEM, NOIR CARME, ZUDANSQUES. Distance 8 miles. Starting time 9.45. Coy & transport arrived ST. MARTIN 13.30. Roads had thawed during the night & no difficulties were experienced. At 13.45 orders were received that Coy less transport would entrain at WATTEN on 6th inst & proceed by rail to YPRES for work under C.E. VIII Corps. Transport to march by road, staging for night 6th/7th at ZERMEZEELE.	
	6		Coy less transport marched to WATTEN, via TILQUES & SERQUES & entrained at WATTEN. Starting time 5.45. Arrived WATTEN 8.30. Train started 9.30. Train arrived YPRES 12.30. Coy marched to camp on CANAL BANK (C 25. d. 4. 5.) arriving there 2.30. Camp consisted of large elephant shelters & was quite satisfactory. Transport marched to HARDIFORT via ST OMER, CLAIRMARAIS, ZUYTPEENE, WEMAERS CAPPEL. Starting time 8.15. Arrived HARDIFORT 15.00. Road was easy & no difficulties occurred.	MAP 28 N.W. 1/20,000
	7		Coy employed on improvements to camp &c. Transport marched to lines at H.16.a.6.6., ½ mile S.E. of VLAMERTINGHE, via OUDEZEELE, WINNEZEELE, WATOU, POPERINGHE, VLAMERTINGHE. Starting time 7.00. Arrived H.16.a.6.6. 15.30. Easy journey, roads being good.	

(A7092). Wt. W12839/M1293. 750,000. 1/17. D. D. & L., Ltd. Forms/C.2118/14.

CONTINUED TO PAGE 3.

Army Form C. 2118.

Instructions regarding War Diaries and Intelligence Summaries are contained in F. S. Regs., Part II. and the Staff Manual respectively. Title pages will be prepared in manuscript.

WAR DIARY of 510TH (LONDON) FIELD COY. R.E.
or
~~INTELLIGENCE SUMMARY.~~ FOR MONTH OF JANUARY 1918.

(Erase heading not required.)

Place	Date	Hour	Summary of Events and Information	Remarks and references to Appendices
B.E.F.	8		Coy employed on camp improvements & reconnaissance of Army Battle Zone (two defensive lines about 2½ miles EAST of YPRES)	
	9		Work as on 8th. Coy (dismounted) had baths in 8th Div bath house on CANAL BANK. Attached for work to C.R.E. 33rd Division	
	10 to 18		Work on Army Battle Zone. The following jobs were carried out: (i) Wiring Machine Gun Rays from M.G. Posts A, B, C, D, E & F. in all about 1200 yds. double apron fence, were put up (ii) Preparation of drainage schemes for UHLAN, RUPPRECHT & GREY KEEPS (map references C.29.b.5.5, C.30.c.3.8. & C.30.d.3.8.) Work was also started on the drainage of these keeps. 4 or 5 drains (av. 100 yds length) being cut at each keep. (iii) Making & marking gaps in front & second wiring systems. About 20 gaps were made good (iv) Reconnaissance of Pill Boxes near SOMME Dressing Station (D.13.b.1.0) & scheme for drainage of Pill Boxes in UHLAN KEEP (C.29.b.5.5) Selection of site for Army Commander's nest of Machine Guns at C.30.b.5.0 (v) General running of RAT FARM SIDING R.E. Dump (C.23.b.7.2)	

(A7092). Wt. W12839/M1293. 750,000. 1/17. D. D. & L., Ltd. Forms/C.2118/14.

CONTINUED TO PAGE 4

Army Form C. 2118.

Instructions regarding War Diaries and Intelligence Summaries are contained in F. S. Regs., Part II. and the Staff Manual respectively. Title pages will be prepared in manuscript.

WAR DIARY of 510TH (LONDON) FIELD COY. R.E.
or
~~INTELLIGENCE SUMMARY.~~ FOR MONTH OF JANUARY 1918.

(Erase heading not required.)

Place	Date	Hour	Summary of Events and Information	Remarks and references to Appendices
B.E.F.	10 to 18		(VI) Making & writing notice boards as under: Type. — Made. Written. Erected 18" x 18" Wooden Boards — 9 — 9 — 8 12" x 9" Tin signs — 80 — 33 — 16	
			(VII) Preparing schemes for conversion & construction of Pill Boxes for use as R.A. O.Ps., Command Posts &c in Army Battle Zone, & organizing 2 dumps for work on above. This was carried out by Capt D. COMINS. R.E.	
	19		Coy again came under orders of C.R.E. 29TH Division, & took over work in back (VLAMERTINGHE) area from 2nd Field Coy. R.E. Work on Army Battle Zone was taken over by 2nd & 15TH Field Coys. R.E. (8TH Division). ½ Company under Lieut W.B. ADAMS. R.E. moved to HOP FACTORY (H.8.a.5.9.) for work in Back Area, H.Q. & 2 Sections remaining at CANAL BANK — starting work on Divl H.Q. (I.1.b.7.8.)	
	20TH To 26		Work in Back Area The following jobs were carried out:— (1) Divl. H.Q. (I.1.b.7.8.) 200 yards double trench board track replaced, 400 yards repaired, relaid & replaced where necessary. Drainage of road approach to D.H.Q. (I.2.b.2.6 – b.1.8.). 12 shelters repaired & fitted (shelving &c) & new work done where required.	

(A7092). Wt. W12839/M1293. 750,000. 1/17. D. D. & L., Ltd. Forms/C.2118/14.

CONTINUED TO PAGE 5.

Army Form C. 2118.

Instructions regarding War Diaries and Intelligence Summaries are contained in F. S. Regs., Part II. and the Staff Manual respectively. Title pages will be prepared in manuscript.

WAR DIARY OF 510TH (LONDON) FIELD COY. R.E.
~~or~~
~~INTELLIGENCE SUMMARY.~~ FOR MONTH OF JANUARY 1918.

(Erase heading not required.)

Place	Date	Hour	Summary of Events and Information	Remarks and references to Appendices
B. E. F.	20 TO 26		(ii) Work on Stabling, VLAMERTINGHE, at G.5.d.2.3., H.8.a.6.6., H.8.a. central, H.9.c.1.6., H.8.a.6.3., Work was continued as far as possible with material available + estimates were got out for further requirements in materials.	
			(iii) Officers' Club VLAMERTINGHE (H.2.d.9.0.) Shelves, tables &c being fitted. Roof repaired	
			(iv) Improving road into BRAKE camp (A.30.c.7.3). Report + estimate of material required made.	
			(v) RED FARM Hospital (G.5.d.8.2). Nissen Hut lined with canvas + stretcher racks being fitted	
			(vi) Notice Boards 24 made + written. Trench Templates 100 made. Artillery Boards 6 made.	
			(vii) 88th Brigade Transport lines RYDE camp G.4.a.6.1. 87th " " " YORK " G.5.b.6.5. Scheme of drainage of above camps got out + forwarded to C.R.E.	
			(viii) Bath House VLAMERTINGHE (H.9.a.4.9.) Scheme for repairs got out.	
			Work on Back Area handed over to 455TH (W. RIDING) Field Coy R.E.	
			Work on Middle Area taken over from 497TH (KENT) Field Coy R.E.	
	27 TO 31		Work on Middle Area.	
			(i) Divl Reserve line s'GRAVENSTAFEL. Drainage scheme for 9 posts of above line was got out, + all drains (in all about 1200 yds of 5' deep drains) were dug by 87TH Bde with R.E. supervision. See map M/3 attached	

(A7092). Wt. W12839/M1293. 750,000. 1/17. D. D. & L., Ltd. Forms/C.2118/14.

CONTINUED TO PAGE 6

Army Form C. 2118.

Instructions regarding War Diaries and Intelligence Summaries are contained in F. S. Regs., Part II. and the Staff Manual respectively. Title pages will be prepared in manuscript.

WAR DIARY of 510th (LONDON) FIELD COY. R.E. or ~~INTELLIGENCE SUMMARY.~~ FOR MONTH OF JANUARY 1918.

(Erase heading not required.)

Place	Date	Hour	Summary of Events and Information	Remarks and references to Appendices
B.E.F.	27 to 31		(ii) 12 new posts to WEST of first (or KOREK) group were sited & drains surveyed for & taped out on the ground.	
			(iii) Breastworks were built round 2 Pill Boxes in Divl reserve line (D.9.C.)	
			(iv) 3 Nissen Huts were erected in ENGLISH CAMP (C.27.C.8.9.)	
			(v) Gas blanketing of dug-outs in WIELTJE was taken in hand	
			(vi) A number of notice boards, templates &c. were made at Coy H.Q.	
			General notes:	
			Effective strength of Unit — Officers / Other Ranks	
			A.F.B 213 dated 29-12-17 — 8 / 187	
			" " " 26-1-18 — 8 / 199	
			Casualties during above period.	
			Evacuated sick — - / 5	
			Transferred — - / 2	
			Reinforcements — - / 19	

(A7092). Wt. W12839/M1293. 750,000. 1/17. D. D. & L., Ltd. Forms/C.2118/14.

CONTINUED TO PAGE 7

Army Form C. 2118.

Instructions regarding War Diaries and Intelligence Summaries are contained in F. S. Regs., Part II. and the Staff Manual respectively. Title pages will be prepared in manuscript.

WAR DIARY OF 510TH (LONDON) FIELD COY. R.E.
or
~~INTELLIGENCE SUMMARY.~~ FOR MONTH OF JANUARY 1918

(Erase heading not required.)

Place	Date	Hour	Summary of Events and Information	Remarks and references to Appendices
			Honours received during month.	
			A/Major B.J. RYAN. R.E.T. awarded M.C. Aut: C.R.E. 29th Div., No: 35/38 d/8-1-18	
			Capt. D. COMINS. R.E. awarded M.C. Aut: 29th Div. No: 80/92 d/1-1-18.	
			548494 A/Corpl. DOWNES. W. } Awarded Military Medal { Authority: 29th Division no. 80/92 d/1-1-18.	
			445371 Sapper BERRY. L.	
			548381 L/Cpl. WARD. G.A.	
			548105 Sapper ELVEY. F.W.	
			548240 Corpl. HINWOOD. H.	
			532371 Sapper RALPH. W.G.	

J.A. Parker
MAJOR, R.E.
O.C. 510th. (LONDON) FIELD COY R.E.

Sketch Plan of Drainage.

DIVL. RESERVE LINE.

S' GRAVENSTAFEL.

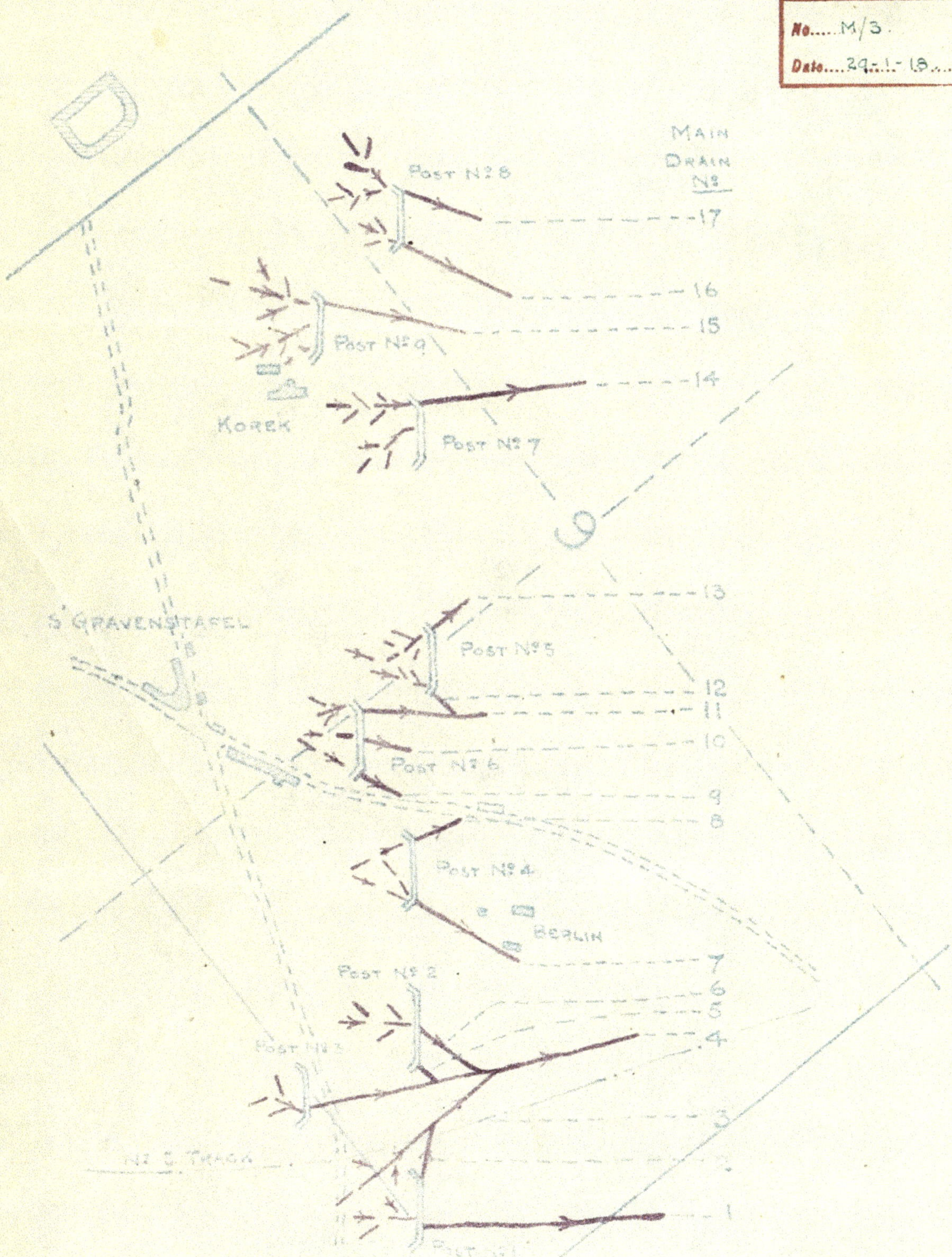

SCALE 1:5,000.

7

CONFIDENTIAL.

WAR DIARY.

of

510th (London) Field Coy R.E.

From 1/2/18. to 28/2/18.

VOLUME. XIX.

Vol 20

Army Form C. 2118.

Instructions regarding War Diaries and Intelligence Summaries are contained in F. S. Regs., Part II. and the Staff Manual respectively. Title pages will be prepared in manuscript.

WAR DIARY OF 510TH (LONDON) FIELD COY R.E.
or
~~INTELLIGENCE SUMMARY.~~ FOR MONTH OF FEBRUARY 1918.
(Erase heading not required.)

Place	Date	Hour	Summary of Events and Information	Remarks and references to Appendices
B.E.F.	1 to 2		Work on Middle Area, Left Divl. Sector, VIII Corps front, continued.	
	3		Took over work on Forward Area from 497th (KENT) Field Coy R.E. & handed over Middle Area to same Coy.	
	3 to 11		Details of work carried out by or under the supervision of 510th (LONDON) Field Coy R.E. as follows:-	
			(1) BELLEVUE Defences	
			Post No. 1. Second task dug, & 75% of post A framed & revetted.	
			Post No. 2 } Post No. 3 } Digging of second task 80-90% completed.	
			Post No. 4. Second task dug & 50% of post A framed & revetted.	
			(2) Pill Box 83 - INCH HOUSES extension of BELLEVUE line	
			Posts 8-12 sited approx as under:	
			Post No. 8 — D. 4. a. 8. 5.	
			9 — D. 4. a. 55. 90.	
			10 — V. 28. c. 0. 4.	
			11 — D. 3. b. 9. 8.	
			12 — D. 3. b. 30. 75.	
			(3) Maintenance work & repairs to tracks No. 5 & 6, MOUSETRAP track & CLUSTER track forward of BELLEVUE. Much work is still required.	

(A7092). Wt. W12839/M1293. 750,000. 1/17. D. D. & L., Ltd. Forms/C.2118/14.

CONTINUED TO PAGE 2.

Army Form C. 2118.

Instructions regarding War Diaries and Intelligence Summaries are contained in F. S. Regs., Part II. and the Staff Manual respectively. Title pages will be prepared in manuscript.

WAR DIARY of 510TH (LONDON) FIELD COY. R.E.
~~or INTELLIGENCE SUMMARY.~~ FOR MONTH OF FEBRUARY 1918.

(Erase heading not required.)

Place	Date	Hour	Summary of Events and Information	Remarks and references to Appendices
B.E.F.	3 TO 11		(4) Preparing formation for Trenchboard Track from MALLARD CROSS roads to No 5 track. Track could not be laid as stores not available at WATERLOO Dump owing to great demand for revetting material &c.	
			(5) Pumping out & cleaning a Pill Box at approx D 4 b 25.05 Work about 50% completed.	
			(6) Siting, taping & preparing drainage schemes for 5 posts on WATERLOO - KRONPRINZ line, also assisting Pioneers in siting wiring. Locations of 5 posts approx as under -	
			Post W.13 D 9 b 3.7	
			W.14 D 3 d 2.4	
			W.15 D.3 d. 0.7	
			W.16 D 3 c. 8.9	
			W.17 D 3 a 25.10	
			(7) Making & writing Notice Boards for Front Line Posts - 60 boards made.	
			(8) Work on erecting Baby Elephant shelters at KRONPRINZ FARM & at WATERLOO. Officers have also visited Battns. on all possible occasions to give any assistance required in work, stores required &c.	
	11		Relieved by 2nd Field Coy. R.E., 8th Division. Coy moved by bus back to WATOU area to rest billets, H.Q. at L.10 a.4.5. Transport at L.14 b 9.4. Coy Camp at CANAL BANK was handed over to II Corps, & Transport lines, VLAMERTINGHE, to 15th Field Coy R.E. 8th Division.	

(A7092). Wt. W12839/M1293 750,000. 1/17. D. D. & L., Ltd. Forms/C.2118/14.

CONTINUED TO PAGE 3

Army Form C. 2118.

WAR DIARY OF 510TH (LONDON) FIELD COY R.E.
or
~~INTELLIGENCE SUMMARY.~~ FOR MONTH OF FEBRUARY 1918.

(Erase heading not required.)

Instructions regarding War Diaries and Intelligence Summaries are contained in F. S. Regs., Part II. and the Staff Manual respectively. Title pages will be prepared in manuscript.

Place	Date	Hour	Summary of Events and Information	Remarks and references to Appendices
B.E.F.	12 TO 28		Rest & training. During this period from 20-28 men were detached from the Coy. being attached to various other units to assist in & supervise camp construction & repair works. Remainder of Coy. was employed on training, refitting, repairing & repainting wagons & on odd jobs generally. Short hours were worked, no afternoon parades being held.	
	27		Instructor from 87th Inf Bde. began the training of 1 N.C.O. & 7 men with the Lewis Gun. Major J.A. PARKER went on a months leave to England. Capt. D COMINS R.E. acting O.C.	

General Notes for Month.

Effective strength of Unit	Officers	O.R.
A.F.B. 213 d/ 26-1-18	8	199
" d/ 23-2-18	8	200

Casualties during above period

	Officers	O.R.
Wounded.	1	—
Evacuated	—	6
Transferred	1	2
Reinforcements	2	9

D Comins
CAPT. ~~MAJOR~~, R.E.
O.C. 510th. (LONDON) FIELD COY R.E.

(A7092). Wt. W12839/M1293. 750,000. 1/17. D. D. & L., Ltd. Forms/C.2118/14.

C O N F I D E N T I A L

W A R   D I A R Y.

of

510th (LONDON) FIELD COY. R.E.

From. 1. 3. 18. To. 31. 3. 18

VOLUME No. 21

Army Form C. 2118.

Instructions regarding War Diaries and Intelligence Summaries are contained in F. S. Regs., Part II. and the Staff Manual respectively. Title pages will be prepared in manuscript.

WAR DIARY of 510th (London) Field Coy R.E.

~~or~~

~~INTELLIGENCE SUMMARY.~~ for Month of March 1918

(Erase heading not required.)

Place	Date	Hour	Summary of Events and Information	Remarks and references to Appendices
B.E.F.	1		Coy at rest billets WATOU Area. HQ at L.10.a.4.5. Transport at L.14.b.9.4. Lecture on the Lewis Gun & extended order drill. Sports ground prepared	
	2		Sports started but had to be abandoned owing to weather. Div band was present.	
	3		Church Parade. Lewis Gun firing practice. No 3 Section won final of inter-section football cup.	
	4		Gas drill & extended order drill.	
	5		Packing & washing wagons. Sports completed in afternoon. No 2 Section won sports cup.	
	6		Coy marched to LOCK Camp I.1.d.8.8., DEAD END. Transport to VLAMERTINGHE, H.8.b.95.95.	
	7		Back Area work taken over from 2nd Field Coy R.E. 8th Division.	
	8 to 12		The following jobs were carried out:–	
			(i) Aid Post ST JEAN. I.3.a.7.8. Elephant shelter erected & sandbagged. Seats windows &c fitted	
			(ii) 2 Nissen Huts erected at I.7.a.4.5.	
			(iii) Concert Hut erected at G.6.c.1.7. & afterwards taken down & packed on site.	
			(iv) Stables at HAGLE Dump. 2 Stables 72' x 24' erected & roofed	
			(v) Crows-nest O.P. erected up a tree at Div H.Q.	

(A7092). Wt. W12839/M1293. 750,000. 1/17. D. D. & L., Ltd. Forms/C.2118/14.

CONTINUED TO PAGE 2

Instructions regarding War Diaries and Intelligence Summaries are contained in F. S. Regs., Part II. and the Staff Manual respectively. Title pages will be prepared in manuscript.

WAR DIARY of 510TH (London) Field Coy R.E. — Army Form C. 2118.

~~or~~

~~**INTELLIGENCE SUMMARY.**~~ for Month of March 1918

(Erase heading not required.)

Place	Date	Hour	Summary of Events and Information	Remarks and references to Appendices
B E F	8 TO 12		(VI) Nissen Hut erected for M.O., R.E. Space between inner + outer lining filled with bricks.	
			(VII) Making + painting notice boards &c.	
	13		Took over forward area work from 497 (Kent) Field Coy R.E.	
	13 TO 29		The following jobs were carried on –	
			(I) 8 Posts WATERLOO Line.	
			(II) C.T. ABRAHAM HEIGHTS.	
			(III) Aid Post GRAVENSTAFEL.	
			(IV) Concreting Bde. H.Q. Pill Box BELLEVUE.	
			(V) C.T. PASSCHENDAELE.	
			(VI) MOSSELMARKT Posts.	
			(VII) BELLEVUE Post.	
			(VIII) Gas Proofing dug-outs &c in KANSAS HOUSE + WIELTJE areas.	
	24		1 Section working under O.i/c Army Battle Zone on strong points &c.	
	30		Forward work handed over to 455 (West Riding) Field Coy R.E. + back area work taken over. Major J.A. PARKER R.E. rejoined Unit.	
	31		2 Sections working under O i/c Army Battle Zone on strong points &c.	
			Other jobs carried on as under	
			(i) Divl Stables at I.1.d.88.	
			(ii) Brigade Transport Lines.	
			(iii) Cinema Hut at BRANDHOEK.	

(A7092). Wt. W12839/M1293. 750,000. 1/17. D. D. & L., Ltd. Forms/C.2118/14.

CONTINUED TO PAGE 3.

Army Form C. 2118.

Instructions regarding War Diaries and Intelligence Summaries are contained in F. S. Regs., Part II. and the Staff Manual respectively. Title pages will be prepared in manuscript.

WAR DIARY of 510th (London) Field Coy R.E.
~~or~~
~~INTELLIGENCE SUMMARY.~~ for Month of March 1918.

(Erase heading not required.)

Place	Date	Hour	Summary of Events and Information			Remarks and references to Appendices
			General notes for month			
			Effective strength of Unit.	Officers	Other ranks	
			A.F.B. 213 dated 23-2-18	8	200	
			A.F.B. 213 dated 30-3-18	7	196	
			Casualties during above period.			
			Wounded	-	1	
			Evacuated	-	11	
			Transferred	1	7	
			Reinforcements		15	

J. R. Packer (?)
MAJOR, R.E.
O.C. 510th. (LONDON) FIELD COY R.E.

(A7092). Wt. W12839/M1293. 750,000. 1/17. D. D. & L., Ltd. Forms/C.2118/14.

29th Divisional Engineers

510th (London) FIELD COMPANY R.E.

APRIL 1918.

C O N F I D E N T I A L

****

Haegedoorne
Pont d'Nieppe
Keersebrom
Croix de Poperinghe

W A R   D I A R Y.

13 K. p. 34.39

of

510TH (LONDON) FIELD COY. R.E.

From..1.4/18.. To..30.4/18...

VOLUME No..22.....

Vol 22

510th (London) Field Coy. RE

Army Form C. 2118.

Instructions regarding War Diaries and Intelligence Summaries are contained in F. S. Regs., Part II. and the Staff Manual respectively. Title pages will be prepared in manuscript.

WAR DIARY
or
INTELLIGENCE SUMMARY.
(Erase heading not required.)

Place	Date	Hour	Summary of Events and Information (Sheet 28 NW I 23 d.9.9)	Remarks and references to Appendices
B.E.F.	April 1st		Company billeted on YPRES Canal Bank. Work on Back Areas i.e. Erection of Stables, & Nissen Huts on top of Plank Road halfway between Canal Bank & VLAMERTINGHE. Erection of Nissen Huts at ENGLISH FARM CAMP & shelters at GODLEY Road	
	2nd to 8th		Company took over Kent Field Coy Billets at YPRES. Work on Army Battle Line Defences. Later Company took over part of work from 33rd Divn. This work consisted of completion of posts on the line CREST FARM – SEINE.	
	9th		Company moved to Brake Camp (Sheet 28 NW Belgium 1/10000 B.30.d.0.3.	

(A7092). Wt. W12539/M1293. 750,000. 1/17. D. D. & L., Ltd. Forms/C.2118/14.

8BR

Instructions regarding War Diaries and Intelligence Summaries are contained in F. S. Regs., Part II. and the Staff Manual respectively. Title pages will be prepared in manuscript.

WAR DIARY
or
INTELLIGENCE SUMMARY.
(Erase heading not required.)

Army Form C. 2118.

Place	Date	Hour	Summary of Events and Information	Remarks and references to Appendices
B.E.F.	APRIL 10th		Coy. Debussed at VIEUX BERQUIN at 6-30 AM & proceeded to billets on the N.W. side of MERVILLE.	
	11th		at 8-30 AM. an order given for Coy to "STAND TO" & 20 men from each section was ordered to proceed to Dig STRONG Points Sheet 36a NE K 30. While doing so the enemy became very active & the sappers had to man the posts which they did excellently. Major Parker Wounded 11th 4.18	
	12th		They were ordered to withdraw owing to flanks giving way but again they organized a line & fought splendidly for 24 hrs they kept the enemy at bay fighting from House to House until relieved at 6.0 AM. on the 13th by 15 Div.	
	13th		During this period in the line the Coy lost 4 Officers Wounded 3 Sappers Killed & 12 Wounded.	
	14th		Coy Hdqrs at ST SYLVESTRE Cappel. Lt Wilson Rejoined Coy from C.R.E. Office.	
	15th		Sappers reporting back to company in small numbers Lt Meffet rejoined Coy at 3 P.M. C.R.E orders Sappers to have a good Rest & good food for 2 days.	[illegible]

(A7092). Wt. W12839/M1293. 750,000. 1/17. D. D. & L., Ltd. Forms/C.2118/14.

Instructions regarding War Diaries and Intelligence Summaries are contained in F. S. Regs., Part II. and the Staff Manual respectively. Title pages will be prepared in manuscript.

WAR DIARY
or
INTELLIGENCE SUMMARY.
(Erase heading not required.)

Army Form C. 2118.

Place	Date	Hour	Summary of Events and Information	Remarks and references to Appendices
BŒ.7	16th		Coy Reorganised ready for work again. New Line South of Castre Laid out Ready for Work at night. 4 Sections at Work on Reserve Line with 500 29 Div Infantry	
	17th		FRont Switch at Rouge Croix. Taped out. and work commenced at night. 4 Section at Work on above line also 500 29 Div Infantry 60 cubic feet Task.	
	18th		Sappers still reporting back to company having got mixed up with other Infantry Battalions while in the line. Work as usual on Rough Croix line South of Castre. Handing over Report prepared & Ready for CRE on 19th Inst. Orders to take over new Work on 2nd Zone Defences. Support & Switch line. from Australian Div.	
				[illegible]

(A7092). Wt. W12839/M1293. 750,000. 1/17. D. D. & L., Ltd. Forms/C.2118/14.

Instructions regarding War Diaries and Intelligence Summaries are contained in F. S. Regs., Part II. and the Staff Manual respectively. Title pages will be prepared in manuscript.

WAR DIARY
or
INTELLIGENCE SUMMARY.
(Erase heading not required.)

Army Form C. 2118.

Place	Date April	Hour	Summary of Events and Information	Remarks and references to Appendices
B. E. F.	19th	-	Company moved from ST. SYLVESTRE - CAPPEL to HONDGEHEM AREA. Capt. S. B. Keast R.E. joined 29th Division & posted O.C. 510th Field Coy. R.E.	
	20th	-	Sappers + 750 Infantry working on 2nd Line Support Line between V. 11. c. 0. 0 + D. 11. b. Central Sheets 27 S.E. + 36A. N.E. 1/20000. O.C. went over above portion of line with C.R.E.	
	21st	-	1100 Infantry working as for 20th. Sappers Hedge thinning. C.R.E.'s Conference	
	22nd	-	600 Infantry working as for 21st. 550. Infantry working on Switch Line from V 30. d. 4 0 to D. 6. a. 9 0. - This work was taped out by O.C. + 2nd Lt Dodd before working Parties arrived. O.C. went over new piece of Support Line to be constructed between V. 23. b. 4. 6 to V. 23. a. 6 2 via V. 24. c. 1. 9. Sappers wiring from V. 11. c. 0. 0. in front of Support Line to V. 17. a. 2. 8 + thinning Hedges in D. 6. b. in front of Switch Line. Capt. S. B. Keast R.E. made Acting Major. C.R.E. R.O. d. 22. 4. 18.	
	23rd	-	350 Infantry working on Support Line V. 17. c. 9. 9. to V. 17. d. 2. 2. Completed. 160 on same Line V. 17. d. 2 2. to V. 23. b. 6. 7. 330 Infantry on Support Line Switch. 350 Infantry on Switch Line. Sappers wiring in Canal + thinning Hedges. Transport obtaining wiring material from Div. Dump + transporting to forward dumps	SBK

(A7092). Wt. W12839/M1293. 750,000. 1/17. D. D. & L., Ltd. Forms/C.2118 14.

Army Form C. 2118.

WAR DIARY
or
INTELLIGENCE SUMMARY.
(*Erase heading not required.*)

Instructions regarding War Diaries and Intelligence Summaries are contained in F. S. Regs., Part II. and the Staff Manual respectively. Title pages will be prepared in manuscript.

Place	Date April	Hour	Summary of Events and Information	Remarks and references to Appendices
B.E.F.	24th		Working Parties Support Line between V.11.c.0.0 & V23.b.6.7 No 300. On Support Switch & wiring same 350. Switch Line 350. Sappers wiring in Stream & Hedges in front of Support Sw. Tch & Thinning Hedges in front of Switch CRE inspected Support Switch & Switch II Lieuts. RUDDOCK & DIXON joined for duty as Sect. Officers & posted to Nos 1 & 2 Sects. respectively.	
	25th		Working Parties as for previous day & on work on Support - Support Switch & Switch Line. Sappers & Infantry wiring Stream. Sappers bridging behind Switch Line & Loop holing Farms behind Support Line CRE. Conference 6 p.m. re taking over Line from 31st Divn. Lieut. Godfrey joined unit as 2/c.	
	26th		Working Parties & Sappers on II Line Support - Support Switch & Switch Line. Trench Constn. Wiring. Drainage. & Loopholing & Sandbagging Bldgs. Round Line with O.C. 210th Field Coy. & to see billets of 211th Fld Coy. Capts for new Horse Lines & Dumps.	
	27th		Sappers working on II Line Defences. Section Officers taken round Line & shown their work for commencing on 28th inst. Coy. H.Qrs moved to D.17.a.1.1. & Horse Lines to D.8.b.2.9.	

Instructions regarding War Diaries and Intelligence Summaries are contained in F. S. Regs., Part II. and the Staff Manual respectively. Title pages will be prepared in manuscript.

WAR DIARY
or
INTELLIGENCE SUMMARY.
(Erase heading not required.)

Army Form C. 2118.

Place	Date April	Hour	Summary of Events and Information	Remarks and references to Appendices
B.E.F.	28th		No. 1 Section Wiring Support Line	
			No. 2 Section ditto + Collecting material for night wiring with Infantry Working Party	
			No. 3 Section Block at J.6.b.4.8. – Construction of Huts in Wood.	
			No. 4 Section Repair of Road D.30.b.5.3. to D.30.b.95.80	
			Improvement of Track X. F.19.d.1.1. to E.27.d.2.1.	
			2nd Lt. Wilson took over Bridges + Trees prepared for Demolition & relieved 497th Kent Fld. Coy. Sappers by (London). Lieut. T.T. Godfrey – made A/Capt.	
	29th		No. 1 Section Wiring Support Line Front Face	
			No. 2 " Night wiring " South Face	
			No. 3 " Block Const. – Huts in Wood – + Advanced Batt. H.Q. Shelter	
			No. 4 " Continuation of Track X.	
			Setting out Track No. 1. from E.25.b.25.95. to E.21.c.0.5.	
	30th		No. 1 Section Wiring Support Line Front Face – Widening – Thickening old wire + forming Apron	
			No. 2 " " " South Face Night work 400x done.	
			No. 3 " Block Continuation – Huts rendering Splinter proof – Advd. Batt. H.Q. Const.	
			No. 4 " On Track X + No. 1. Clearing – Improving + Bridging.	
			Charges in Bridges increased to 50% overcharge for Hasty Demolition. 3 Foot Bridges prepared for Demolition. 2 Lorry loads Road Metal obtained for repairs to LAMOTTE – RUE DE BOIS Road.	

G. Banks Kent
MAJOR, R.E.
O.C. 510th (LONDON) FIELD COY. R.E.

(A7092). Wt. W12839/M1293. 750,000. 1/17. D. D. & L., Ltd. Forms/C.2118/14.

CONFIDENTIAL

WAR DIARY.

of

510th (LONDON) Fd Coy R.E.

From 1/5/18 To 31/5/18

VOLUME No. XXIII

Vol 23

Volume 23

510th (London) Field Coy. R.E.

Instructions regarding War Diaries and Intelligence Summaries are contained in F. S. Regs., Part II. and the Staff Manual respectively. Title pages will be prepared in manuscript.

WAR DIARY
or
INTELLIGENCE SUMMARY.
(Erase heading not required.)

Army Form C. 2118.

Place	Date	Hour	Summary of Events and Information	Remarks and references to Appendices
B 2 F	May. 1		No Infantry Working Parties No 1 Section Wiring - Support Line - East Face. No 2 Section Wiring Support Line - South Face - Night Work. No 3 Section Coy H Qrs Huts at E 26 Central + Road Block - LA MOTTE - RUE DE BOIS Road. No 4 Section Communication Trench X + No 1. Conference of O.C. Coys with the C.R.E. at Head Quarters - 2.30 pm	
	2nd.		Round Line with C.R.E. re defence of left of Brigade + wiring in Wood. Infantry Parties 120 by Day + 120 by Night. Work as for 1st.	
	3rd		Infantry Parties 120 strong only. Work as for 2nd - only No 2 Sect on Day work completing back apron of wire in S. Face of Wood. New Scheme for Demolitions instituted. This Coy in charge of Right Brigade Forward Group. II Lt R.S. Dodd put in charge with 1 N.C.O. + 5 Sappers. II Lt W. Wilson - evacuated - Jas. Battle sent to him in LA MOTTE.	
	4th		Casualty. No 1 Sect. Night Wiring. S Face Wood between E.27 d. 3.0 + E 27. d. 7 2. No 2 Sect Preparing Line for Wiring K 3. a. 1. 6 to K. 2. b. 6. 5. + Carrying No 3 Sect. Coy H Qrs - T.M.B. H.Q. - Block + transporting stores for Battn H.Q. No 4 Sect. Communication Trench X No 1 + 4. Infantry 270. Demolition Party started Mine at D. 30. d. 05. 70. + Making Notice Boards.	S.B.R.

Instructions regarding War Diaries and Intelligence Summaries are contained in F. S. Regs., Part II. and the Staff Manual respectively. Title pages will be prepared in manuscript.

WAR DIARY
or
INTELLIGENCE SUMMARY.

(Erase heading not required.)

Army Form C. 2118.

Place	Date	Hour	Summary of Events and Information	Remarks and references to Appendices
[illegible]	5th		No1 Section - [illegible] wiring [illegible]	
			No2 Section Preparing & Setting out trail for new Defended locality at E.20 Central	
			No3 Section T.M.B. HQrs - Battn HQrs - [illegible] Block	
			No4 Section - Communication Track X No 1&2	
			Demolition Party [illegible] [illegible] & making & painting Notice Bds.	
	6th		No1 Sect. Wiring Support line - thickening - widening & clearing in front of line. Night preparing Road Mine at E.28.c.3.3	
			No2 Sect. Work on Defended Locality E.20.c Wiring & digging Posts & thinning Hedge	
			No3 Sect. Camouflaging R Support Coy HQ - T.M.B. HQ Splinterproofing - 2 Battn HQ. erecting Shelters. Block - revetting - wiring & thinning hedge	
			No4 Sect. Communication Track No1 X 1&2 Bridging	
			Demolition Party. Mining & making Notice Boards	
	7th		No1 Sect. Wiring Support line - No2 Sect. on Defended Locality (150 Men Reserve Battn)	
			No3 Sect. Sp[illegible]proofing Coy. HQ - T.M.B. HQrs - 2 Battn HQrs. Sandbagging Shelters - Block.	
			No4 Sect. Tracks X 1&2. - Reconnoitred line of wire - East Defence of Wood.	
			Demolition Party. Mining & Making Notice Bds.	
	8th		Road Mine at E.28.c.3.3. Destroyed 3 a.m. [illegible]	
			No1 Sect. with 110 Infy Started wiring Right flank M.G. [illegible] East of Wood.	
			No2 on Defended Locality E.20 Central. No3 Sect. Battn HQ & Block	
			No4 Communication Tracks No1 X 1&2	

Instructions regarding War Diaries and Intelligence Summaries are contained in F. S. Regs., Part II. and the Staff Manual respectively. Title pages will be prepared in manuscript.

WAR DIARY
or
INTELLIGENCE SUMMARY.
(Erase heading not required.)

Army Form C. 2118.

Place	May Date	Hour	Summary of Events and Information	Remarks and references to Appendices
B.E.F.	9th		Round works with C.R.E. - Road mine at E.28.c.3.3. fired 1 a.m.	
			No 1 Section. Wiring Support line + Clearing 20" wide - in front of Right Ray. M.G. line.	
			No 2 " Defended Locality at E.20 Central	
			No 3 2 Battn H.Qrs + Block	
			No 4 Communication No 1 + 4 Tracks	
			Heavy gas shell bombardment around billets - night 8/9th.	
	10th		Work as for 9th. Garrison of E.20 Central started work on Locality.	
			Reconnoitred BOURRE RIVER LINE with IInd Lt MEFFET. + selected Posts.	
			IInd Lt DODD + MEFFET awarded M.Cs.	
			Heavy gas shell bombardment around billets. Night 10/11th.	
	11th		Owing to heavy shelling of LE TIR ANGLAIS - Coy H.Qrs moved to D.9.c.3.2. Move started 4.30pm - Completed 6.30 pm	
			Work on Line No 1 Sect: Wiring M.G. Ray + Coy H.Q. started at (Infy 60+80)	
			No 2 " E.20 Central. Cont. of wiring Garrison 45 + 30 (R.D.F.)	
			No 3 " 2 Battn and Infy + Coy H.Q. at K.2.b.5.6 started.	
			No 4 Tracks 1+4 Bridge Foot Tracks at E.25.d.30.95 BOURRE River Defences started - but working party of 2nd R Battn Unable	
	12th		Work on Line as for 11th. Some sappers kept in camp to erect shelters etc.	
			Total Casualties from Gas Bombardment of Nights 8/9th + 10/11th = 19	
	13th		Work on Line as for 12th plus night work making Cellar at K.3.d.4.2 in Coy H.Q. Reinforcements joined Company Part	
			6 Tunnelling Coy: R.E. attached for Rations + for work making Hurdles etc Bois d'Amont	

(A7092). Wt. W12839/M1293. 750,000. 1/17. D. D. & L., Ltd. Forms/C.2118/14.

Instructions regarding War Diaries and Intelligence Summaries are contained in F. S. Regs., Part II. and the Staff Manual respectively. Title pages will be prepared in manuscript.

WAR DIARY
or
INTELLIGENCE SUMMARY.
(Erase heading not required.)

Army Form. C. 2118.

Place	Date (May)	Hour	Summary of Events and Information	Remarks and references to Appendices
B E F	14th		No 1 Sect. Nightwork Propping Cellar at CANDESCURE for Coy HQ. Day work. Coy H Qrs wiring M.G. Rays No 2 Sect. Defended Locality E 20 Central Post & wiring No 3 Sect. 2 Battn H.Q. E 25 Central. Coy H.Q. K 2 b central. No 4 Sect. Bridge R BOURRE. Defence R BOURRE. Trench improvement Saw O.C. 'A' Coy 2nd M.G. Bn re wiring M.G. position La Motte ch & arranged Distant work.	
	15th		Only 1 Working Party - 40 Men. Lamp Frontier - wiring M G Rays Company Day off from Line Work. Company Parade 9 a.m. Inspection of [illegible] SAA. Inspection - Work improving Camp 10-1 pm. Latrines - preparing Horse Lines - Shelter Incinerator made - Drivers Kitchen etc.	
	16th		Round Reserve Line. R. Bourre. With CRE re siting of Posts. Sects 1.2.3.4 on work as for 14th. Also No 3 Sect dismantled Hut at Lallorse & blew down Small Hut by Sh. 27 Reinforcements arrived. Horse Lines moved to Same Camp as Coy H Qrs	
	17th		Set out Posts on Reserve Line - R Bourre. Sections on work as for 16th. Reinforcements posted. Met G.O.C. 88th Bde re site for Support Battn HQ & decided on D.24 a 7.7 approx. 1 2nd Cpl. Reinforcement arrived & posted to No 1 Sect.	
	18th		Sections on works as [illegible] No 3 Sect started Support Battn HQ at D.24 a 7.7 & No 4 Section started work on R Bourre Posts - now under charge of CRE. Met Div General along Bourre R & showed him posts. R Bourre lowered 1' by opening [illegible] DAM sluice.	BH

(A7092). Wt. W12839/M1293. 750,000. 1/17. D. D. & L., Ltd. Forms/C.2118/14.

Instructions regarding War Diaries and Intelligence Summaries are contained in F. S. Regs., Part II. and the Staff Manual respectively. Title pages will be prepared in manuscript.

WAR DIARY
or
INTELLIGENCE SUMMARY.
(Erase heading not required.)

Army Form C. 2118.

Place	Date May	Hour	Summary of Events and Information	Remarks and references to Appendices
[illegible]	19th		[illegible] 88th I [illegible] [illegible] on Right [illegible] + 86 [illegible] [illegible] Park. [illegible] [illegible] Batts [illegible]	
			[illegible] No 1 [illegible] M.G. [illegible] + Coy [illegible]	
			No 2 Night [illegible] E 20 [illegible]	
			No 3 [illegible] [illegible] M.G. [illegible]	
			No 4 [illegible]	
	20th		Round E 20 Central [illegible] CRE + Decided [illegible]	
			[illegible] from [illegible] [illegible] [illegible]	
			[illegible] on [illegible] Working [illegible] = 248	
			~~[illegible]~~ Summary of Evidence [illegible] 541223.	
			Spr WILSON [illegible] Charged with [illegible]	
	21st		[illegible] Canal [illegible] CRE – Bridge at K 1 c 6.2 prepared for Demolition taken over from 59th Field Coy 8th Divn Section at work [illegible] Extra Working Party – 97 [illegible] from Reserve Brigade for [illegible]	
			CRE Conference 3 pm To 88th [illegible]	
	22nd		To Site for Battn in the Line HQ [illegible] Trench. Site selected by G.O.C. 88th Bde not good. Set out Posts along Canal. Reserve Line with [illegible] Section on work as above – No 3 Sectn also wiring Railway Bridge at K 1 c 9.4 [illegible] Brigade + received instr to Start work on Battn in Line H.Q. at E 20 a 6.8 + Advd Brigade HQ at D.24 60.95 Dr Lyons + Spr Medway No 3 Sectn wounded	[initials]

(A7092). Wt. W12839/M1293. 750,000. 1/17. D. D. & L., Ltd. Forms/C.2118/14.

Instructions regarding War Diaries and Intelligence Summaries are contained in F. S. Regs., Part II. and the Staff Manual respectively. Title pages will be prepared in manuscript.

WAR DIARY
or
INTELLIGENCE SUMMARY.
(Erase heading not required.)

Army Form C. 2118.

Place	Date May	Hour	Summary of Events and Information	Remarks and references to Appendices
B.E.F.	23rd		Reserve Line - Canal & R. Bourre with Div. Gen & CRE & B.G. - 88th I Bde No. 1 Sect. Wiring M.G. Bay & Coy H.Q. Infantry Party withdrawn owing to shell fire. No. 2 Sect. (Sapper) Nightwork on Battn in Line H.Q. (SMARTENBROUCK). Infantry filling Breastworks of Posts E.20 Central No. 3 Support Battn H.Q. Wiring Rly Bage K.1.c.9.4. Roadline Brick Chamber. Worked up No. 4. Reserve Line No Pioneers turned up for revetting. Infantry on Parapets. 3. Reinforcements joined.	
	24th		Nos. 1. 3 & 1/2 No. 4 Sects Day off. Heavy Rain. Drill & Gas Parade afternoon No. 2 Sects on Nightwork Battn H.Q. Smartenbrouck. No. 4 Sect. Working Party of 100 men & 3 Platoons on Reserve Line. 2/Lt Meffet met Capt. Macaulay re Corps O.P.	
	25th		Work as for 23rd. Visited all jobs. Set out 5th Post on Canal Reserve Line. Went to see Staff re Corps O.P.	
	26th		Set out Wire Ramp along Open Part Reserve Line - R. Bourre Front. No. 1 Sect. Low Wire entanglement E of Support Line. No. 2 Sect. E.20 Central - Breastworks to Posts. - Nightwork Battn in the Line H.Q. SMARTENBROUCK - Elephant Shelter. No. 3 Sect. Support Battn H.Q. - Erecting Camouflage Advd Brigade HQ - La Motte Mine. No. 4 Sect. Posts along Canal Bank excavation & forming Breastworks Canal Reserve Line. 2/Lt Meffet & 5th OMAR Rest Camp. 1. Sapper Reinforcement arrived. Corps O.P.	

518th Field Coy R.E.

Instructions regarding War Diaries and Intelligence Summaries are contained in F. S. Regs., Part II. and the Staff Manual respectively. Title pages will be prepared in manuscript.

WAR DIARY
or
INTELLIGENCE SUMMARY.
(Erase heading not required.)

Army Form C. 2118.

Place	Date (May)	Hour	Summary of Events and Information	Remarks and references to Appendices
B.E.F.	27th		Reserve Line. Setting out M.G. Emp. & Keeps & enfilading Post. To Arcques to see Concrete Battn. H.Q. II Lt. Parsons joined from Base. To E.20 Central – Swartenbrouck – Reserve Line. — Work party from Reserve Brigade. Pioneers revetting Posts. Other work as for 26th. Brigade Cellar strengthening	
	28th		Reserve Line. Revetting Canal Post, Posts between Sawmill & River Junc., Post in Rly & 3 MG Posts Breastworks – post between Rly & Road. Digging Canal Post between Rly & Road. No 4 Section. No 3 Section. Brigade Adv. H.Q. Excavation. Support Battn. H.Q. Splinterproofing. Wiring Rly Bdge. No 2 Section. Right work. Battn. in Line H.Q. Sandbagging shelters. E20 Central completing Post on S. of Road. No 1 Section. Wiring Support Line. Right work. New wire Keeps K.3.b.8.0. to E.27.d.5.0.	
	29th		As for 28th. Plan to 88th Brigade for Concrete Coy. H.Qrs. Pioneers started wiring River Line	
	30th		Work as for 29th. Selecting site for Concrete Block Dug out in E.20 Central	
	31st		No 1 Section on wiring – Keeps etc. E. of Support Line No 2 " a) E.20 Central in Posts b) Battn. H.Q. SWARTENBROUCK No 3 a) Support Battn. H.Q. b) Adv. Brigade H.Q. c) Dug outs PRE à VIN. d) LAMOTTE Road Mine e) Workshops No 4 R. BOURRE Secn. Reserve Line – Wiring & Revetting Posts (Pioneers). Canal Secn. " " Parapets of Posts.	

G Banks Read
MAJOR, R.E.
O.C. 518th (LONDON) FIELD COY. R.E.

(A7092). Wt. W12839/M1293. 750,000. 1/17. D. D. & L., Ltd. Forms/C.2118/14.

CONFIDENTIAL.

****

WAR DIARY

OF

510th(LONDON)FIELD COY.R.E.

FROM

1/6/18 TO 30/6/18.

VOLUME NO.24.

****

Vol 24

Volume 24. 570th Field Coy. R.E.

Instructions regarding War Diaries and Intelligence Summaries are contained in F. S. Regs., Part II. and the Staff Manual respectively. Title pages will be prepared in manuscript.

WAR DIARY
or
~~INTELLIGENCE SUMMARY.~~
(Erase heading not required.)

Army Form C. 2118.

Place	Date	Hour	Summary of Events and Information	Remarks and references to Appendices
B.E.F.	June 1.		23 Reinforcements arrived.	
			No 1 Sect. Wiring M G Rays etc E. of Support Line	
			No 2 Sect. a) E.20 Central - Posts. b) Preparing Site for Concrete Block Dugout c) Line Battn. H.Q Small Elep Lank - SWARTENBROUCK d) Brigade H.Q. Proofing Cellar	
			No 3 Sect. a). Support Battn. H.Q D.24.a.7.1. b) Advd Brigade H.Q D.24 a.65.05. c) Dugouts in Rly Bank PRE à VIN. d) La Motte Road Mine	
			No 4 Sect. a) Reserve Line - R.Bourne Sector Posts Parapets - Wiring. South the end. b.) " " Canal " " "	
			Pioneers. 1 Platoon Wiring Reserve Line - R.Bourne Sector. 1 Platoon Revetting Posts. Corps O.P.	
	2nd		Work as for 1st. except the Pioneers. Attended F.G.C.M. re No 528225 Spr. WILSON A. as witness. Saw 87th Infy Brigade re C.R.E's.	
	3rd		Work as for 2nd. + 1 Platoon Pioneers Wiring River Line + 1 Platoon at PRE à VIN. La MOTTE Bridge Hut - Temp'y repairs executed. To see G.O.C. 87th Infy Bde re work.	
	4th		No Working Parties on E.20. Central or Swartenbrouck. No Reserve Brigade Party on Reserve Line Sapper work + other parties as for 3rd. 87th Infy Brigade relieved 88th in Right Sector. No 1 Section relieved No 3 Section in LAMOTTE.	
	5th		Training Day. RSM Sabine took No 2.3.4 Sects + HQ in Drill with + without Arms. Pioneers 2 Platoons + 60 Men on Reserve Line Wiring + Canal Posts. 40 Men on E.20 Central 40 Men on Support Battn. H.Q. + Advd Brigade H.Q. CSM. Norris? arrived.	S.B.K.

(A7092). Wt. W12839/M1293. 750,000. 1/17. D. D. & L., Ltd. Forms/C.2118/14.

Instructions regarding War Diaries and Intelligence Summaries are contained in F. S. Regs., Part II. and the Staff Manual respectively. Title pages will be prepared in manuscript.

WAR DIARY
or
INTELLIGENCE SUMMARY.
(Erase heading not required.)

Army Form C. 2118.

Place	Date June	Hour	Summary of Events and Information	Remarks and references to Appendices
B.E.F.	6th		Billets shelled with Gas during early morning.	
			No 1 Sectn Repr LAMOTTE Swing Bridge - Support Battn H.Q. - Advd Brigade H.Q. - Workshops.	
			No 2 " E.20 Central - Posts - Preparing site for O.B. D.ment - Battn H.Q. [illegible] Rat in E.20 Central	
			No 3 " Wiring E. of Support Line. Maintenance of La Motte - Rue de Bois Road taken over from No 4 Sectn.	
			No 4 " Reserve Line - 2 Platoon Pioneers wiring. 1 Squad & R.E. wiring. Infantry on Posts.	
	7th		Work as for 6th except that No 3 Sectn started work on reconstruction of Posts - Support Line - Right Battn.	
	8th		As for 7th. With C.R.E. to E.20 Central & Right Battn in the Line Site. No 1 Sectn 2 Sappers shoring Brigade Cellar	
	9th		As for 8th. La Motte Swing Bridge Repairs Completed. No 2 Section started 3 days training. O.P. at D.13.b.7.6 & D.O. at D.13.c Central started.	
	10th		Work as for 9th. No 2 Sectn second days training.	
	11th		No 1 Sectn on work as before. No 2 Sect third days training. No 3 Sectn Improving Posts - Support Line. No 4 Sectn (less 8 men on works) Drill & Map reading. Went up to Line with Brigadier	
	12th		No 1 Sectn as before. - No 2 & 3 Sectn in relief. - Temp Battn H.Q. in E.27.a. No 4 - Making B. Torpedoes & bridges.	

(A7092). Wt. W12839/M1293. 750,000. 1/17. D. D. & L., Ltd. Forms/C.2118/14.

Instructions regarding War Diaries and Intelligence Summaries are contained in F. S. Regs., Part II. and the Staff Manual respectively. Title pages will be prepared in manuscript.

WAR DIARY
or
INTELLIGENCE SUMMARY.
(Erase heading not required.)

Army Form C. 2118.

Place	Date	Hour	Summary of Events and Information	Remarks and references to Appendices
K.2.7.	13th		No 1 Sectn Advd Brigade HQ – a) Making track for Tramway, b) Duckboard track in front of Shelters c) Shifting sand & gravel d) Excavation No 3 Shelter. – Brigade HQ erection of Shelters. Infantry 40 + 15	
			No 2 & 3 Sections. Temp Y HQrs Infy 105 men in 3 Reliefs E.20 Central 1.R.E. 40 Infy	
			No 4 Section Making Bridges & Bangalore Ts in Camp. Pioneers 2 Platoons working Reserve Line	
			Night Work. * Digging Straight Trench E.28.c.05.15 to E.28.c.1.0. & Screening same with branches in parapet. ⊗ Thickening ledge W. side road K.4.a. (* Night 12/13. ⊗ Night 12/13 & 13/14)	
	14th		As for 13th Also worked on Reserve Line Post. 94 Infantry.	
	15th		Camp shelled with H.V. gun about 3 am to 10 am at intervals 1 Horse wounded + 1 Driver killed Shell Slits Dug in evening. Transport moved back to Old transport lines	
			Dug new Trench S. end A. [illegible] to 5th Divn Boundary K.2.b.7.0. Length 600x approx	
			Section on Ordinary Work	
	16th		Sections at work in Camp. Trench quoted in work for 15th inst. connected with night 16/17	
	17		Section Ordinary Work. 30 Extra Bangalore Torpedoes made for Brigade	
	18th		No 1 [illegible] No 2 Draw [illegible] Battn HQ. – [illegible] E.20 Central [illegible] Coy HQrs E.20 Central No 3 Section putting bridges on Sides E. edge of Wood & small DO. Right Temp Y Battn HQ No 4 Section on Tram line – extending S. Spur to E. edge of Wood. Conference 2 pm C.R.E. at W. Ridings. Drafting Operation Orders	
	19th	–	No 1 Section Advd Brigade HQ Demolitions. No 2 Section [illegible] up [illegible] R.E. Dump. E.28.a.42.10. No 3 Section Completing Small D.O. Right Temp Y Battn HQ No 4 Sectn & 2 Platoons Pioneers Tramway. Writing Operation & Administrative Orders.	

(A7092). Wt. W12839/M1293. 750,000. 1/17. D. D. & L., Ltd. Forms/C.2118/14.

8 R.E.

Instructions regarding War Diaries and Intelligence Summaries are contained in F. S. Regs., Part II. and the Staff Manual respectively. Title pages will be prepared in manuscript.

WAR DIARY
or
INTELLIGENCE SUMMARY.
(Erase heading not required.)

Army Form C. 2118.

Place	June Date	Hour	Summary of Events and Information	Remarks and references to Appendices
B.E.F.	20th		Forming Operation Dumps. Handing over Works etc. Major Read to Hospital	
	21st.		Handed over to 211 Field Coy. RE. - Company moved to RACQUINGHEM	
	22nd.		Company cleaning up. Kit Inspection etc.	
	23rd		Company Training. Physical - Lecture Sanitation - Close Order Drill. Map Reading	
	24th		" " " Veterinary. Demolition. - Close Order & Musketry Drill. Setting out work & use of Field level	
	25th		" Fitting M.O. - Guard Mounting - Lecture on Discipline by RSM. Map Reading	
	26th		" Musketry Drill - Close Order Drill by RSM. - Field Sketching. IInd Lt. DIXON to Hospital. No. 1 Sectn. on Range.	
	27th		" Lecture Attack & Defence in Open Warfare - Musketry & Fire Control under RSM - Lecture Sanitation & Hygiene - Major Read returned from Hospital.	
	28th		" Field Sketching Bayonet Fighting.	
	29th		" M.O. Parade under RSM. - NCOs instruction by RSM in drilling a Squad. Packing & cleaning Tool Carts & Limbers	
	30th		" Tool Carts & Wagon Cleaning. Officers & NCOs Lecture by CRE on Reconnaissance. M. Order Inspection Parade by OC on Parade Ground.	SBR

S Banks Read Major RE

(A7092). Wt. W12839/M1293. 750,000. 1/17. D. D. & L., Ltd. Forms/C.2118/14.

Vol 25

CONFIDENTIAL

WAR DIARY

OF

510TH (LONDON) FIELD COY. R.E.

FROM 1-7-18 TO 31-7-18

VOLUME 25.

VOLUME 25. 510th Field Company RE

Army Form C. 2118.

Instructions regarding War Diaries and Intelligence Summaries are contained in F. S. Regs., Part II. and the Staff Manual respectively. Title pages will be prepared in manuscript.

WAR DIARY
or
~~INTELLIGENCE SUMMARY.~~

(Erase heading not required.)

Place	Date 1918 July	Hour	Summary of Events and Information	Remarks and references to Appendices
B.E.F.	1.		Inspection by C.R.E. Full Marching Order. 9 am - 1.30 pm	
	2nd		G.O.C.s Inspection.	
	3rd		9.15 - 10.45 am Whole Coy. Gas Discipline & Instruction 11 am to 1 pm Demolitions - Lecture & Practical for Sappers	
	4th		9 - 10 am Whole Coy. Medical Inspection by M.O. - 10 - 11 am Tool Carts. Musketry - 5 Rounds Grouping - 5 Rds Application - 10 Rounds Rapid - Nos 2 3 & 4 Sects.	
	5th		Drill. ~~[illegible]~~ Instruction in Contents of Tool Carts.	
	5th		Officers & NCOs (Senior) Map Enlargement & fitting in Scheme. Coy: Drill & Demonstration in Setting out Fire & C Trenches & Strong Points.	
	6th		Lecture: Sect. Officers Bridging in Open Warfare. Officers Water Supply Scheme. Work on Sports Ground.	
	7th		R.E. Sports	
	8th		2 Sects. work on Polo Gd. for Dvr. Horse Show. 2 Sect. & Mtd. & H.Q. Baths.	
	9th		Dvr. Horse Show - Holiday	
	10th		Staff Ride - Bridging Scheme for Officers & Senior NCOs - 28 Men Inoculated - 10 Men to Calais by Lorry for Delivery. Remainder Pontooning	
	11th		Company Scheme.	S.B.R.
	12th		Staff Ride Cancelled - Wet. Officers Exercise - Calculation Bridge [illegible] II Lt. COATES joined	

(A7092). Wt. W12839/M1293. 750,000. 1/17. D. D. & L., Ltd. Forms/C.2118/14.

570th Field Coy R.E.

2

Instructions regarding War Diaries and Intelligence Summaries are contained in F. S. Regs., Part II. and the Staff Manual respectively. Title pages will be prepared in manuscript.

WAR DIARY
or
INTELLIGENCE SUMMARY.
(Erase heading not required.)

Army Form C. 2118.

Place	Date	Hour	Summary of Events and Information	Remarks and references to Appendices
	July			
B.E.F.	13		No 1, 2 & 3 Sect. Road Reconnaissances. No 4 Sect. Jas & Rifle Drill & packing wagons	
	14		Company under RSM 2 Hrs Drill	
	15		Staff Ride. Company Jas & Rifle Drill & work in Camp	
	16		Company Scheme.	
	17		Company moved from Camp at RACQUINGHEM to new location in BANDRINGHEM	
	18		Rifles Iron Ration Inspection. Kit Lashings. Marking wagons improving Camp. Lewis Gun Teams instruction	
	19		Rifle Inspection. Lewis Gun Teams Training. Kit & Lashings. Drill - Barbed wire apron fencing	
	20		Officers. Staff Ride (Demolition Scheme R.A.A.). O.C. Position Scheme. Changed Horse Lines to Heath.	
	21st		Rifle Inspection. Church Parade. 2nd Lt. Ruddock left for England to Transportation Branch R.E.	
	22nd		Company moved from BANDRINGHEM to Sheet 27 1:40000. H.15.b.5.3.	
	23rd		Company " H.15.b.5.3 to H.21.c.54.80.	
	24		Rifle Inspection Cleaning Wagons Harness etc.	

[initials]

510th Field Coy R.E.

Instructions regarding War Diaries and Intelligence Summaries are contained in F. S. Regs., Part II. and the Staff Manual respectively. Title pages will be prepared in manuscript.

WAR DIARY
or
INTELLIGENCE SUMMARY.
(Erase heading not required.)

Army Form C. 2118.

Place	Date (July)	Hour	Summary of Events and Information	Remarks and references to Appendices
BEF	25		Company moved from S 27/H 21 c 52.00 to S 27/R 7 a 36.20. Mounted & transport by Road. Dismounted by Lorry	
	26th		Officers work: Reconnaissance. Sappers improving Camp. Coy. Transport NIGHT - transporting Stores to R 24 c 3.1 for Dugout accom.	
	27th		3 Sections in 2 Reliefs on 2 Bn HQ (Battn) at R 24 c 3.1 - c 6.7. Stores to Corps OPERATION Dumps at S/27 R 22 c 75.55 & S 28/M 15 a 50.60 (Right Bank) (6 loads). 1 Section forming & camouflaging Dumps	
	28th		Same as for 27th. Instructions recd. to make Splinter proof Shelters for 2 men at Dumps.	
	29th		Cont. of work. Splinter proof Shelters at 2 Dumps Commenced. To LACLOCHE & LE MOIR PILL BOX to X Corps H A reconn. for same	
	30th		Work as for 29th. Reconnoitred Site for Mona Pill Box OP. for X Corps H A with Staff but on Mont NOIR. Orders received to prepare & move on 31st - later postponed to 1st prox.	
	31st		Parade - Fresh Air.	S. Beakbane[?] Major R.E.

510th Field Coy: RE

COMPANY SCHEME. 11/7/18
****

General Idea.

The Germans have launched a heavy offensive South Westwards across the line of the St.Omer _ Aire Canal and have turned our Left Flank.

The Division is retiring along ROQUETOIRE - MAMETZ and ROQUETOIRE - REBECQ Roads.

G.O.C. has decided that the Rear Guard shall offer strong resistence along the high ground to South of the River LYS. In order to get the Main Guard across the River, certain Strong Points along the line REBECQ - RINCQ Road must be held.

S Banks Keen Major RE

SPECIAL IDEA. (Map Ref: Sheet 36A. 1:40000)

In order to facilitate the execution of Plan laid down in General Idea - G.O.C. has instructed C.R.E. to carry out certain work - i.e. Preparation for Demolition of Road Bridges over River LA LYS at Northern entrances to MAMETZ and CRECQUES, and defence of Wood, North of REBECQ - RINCQ Road in Square G.23.d. Also defences along High Ground, South of River LYS in Square G.28.c.

C.R.E. has detailed 510th. Field Coy to carry out above work.

O.C. No.1 Section.

~~You will proceed with your~~ Your Section ~~and~~ will tape out Postson high ground - commanding River LYS in Square G.28.c.

The piece of front in question will be held by 3 Platoons (Average Strength of 1 Platoon, 25Men + 2 Lewis Guns.)

Garrison will probably arrive at these Posts at 5.30.p.m.- Posts must be ready for occupation by this time.

Indents for Working Parties to be sent in to O.C. ~~510th.Field Coy~~ at Tany. C.H.Q. at Cross Roads. G.23.c.4.5. as early as possible.

Sappers will get all Tools necessary on Site of Work to carry on until Working Party arrives. (Actually Sappers will not dig nor cut hedges.)

Coy will Rendezvous for return to Camp at G.16.d. 2.9.(NATOY FARM.) at 4.0.p.m.

Sketch of Works and report on other Work that you would carry out in connection with this Scheme to be delivered to O.C. 510th.Field Coy at above Rendezvous.

O.C. No.2 Section.

You will prepare for demolition the Road Bridge over River LYS at N entrance to CRECQUES.

All charges used will be dummy - but real primers and detonators will be used.

The charge will be blown by Field Coy with Rear Guard, who should arrive during the afternoon.

After job has been inspected, you will Rendezvous for return to Camp at G.16.d.2.9. (NATOY FARM) by 4.0 p.m.

Sketch showing dimensions of Bridge and calculations will be ready to hand over to incoming Coy.

O.C. No.3 Section.

You will prepare Wood on North side of REBECQ - RINCQ Road in Square G.23.d. for the Rear Guard to Defend.

Tape out Defences and get necessary tools that will be required by Sappers on to the job.

Indents for Working Parties to be delivered to O.C. at Cross Roads -G.23.c.4.5. as early as possible

Garrison (2 Platoons + 4 Lewis Guns) will probably arrive to take over Defences at about 5.0 p.m. and all work must be completed by this time. (Actually no digging or hedge cutting will be carried out.)

Coy will Rendezvous for return to Camp at G.16. d.2.9.(NATOY FARM.) at 4.0.p.m.

Sketches of Works and report showing other Work you would carry out in connection with Scheme to be delivered to O.C. at above Rendezvous at 4.0.p.m.

O.C. No. 4 Section.

You will prepare for demolition the Road Bridge over River LYS at N entrance to MAMETZ.

All charges used will be dummy - but real primers and detonators will be used.

The charge will be blown by Field Coy with Rear Guard, who should arrive during the afternoon.

After job has been inspected, you will Rendezvous for return to Camp at G.16.d.2.9. (NATOY FARM) by 4.0 p.m.

Sketch showing dimensions of Bridge and calculations will be ready to hand over to incoming Coy.

Company Scheme 16/7/18 Map Ref S.36A N.E.

General Idea.

Enemy have been driven back from the line of the AIRE - St.OMER Canal Southwards and have retired across the R. LA LYS. 29th. Division in pursuit on the front REBECQ (inclusive) - GLOMENGHEM (exclusive).

510th. Field Company, marching with 86th. I. Bde. - less 1 Section with Advance Guard of ½ Battn. Enemy have destroyed all bridges across the LYS.

Cavalry have managed to cross R. LYS and form a screen on S. side of River.

River too deep for Infantry to ford.

Special Idea.

Division is advancing by roads - ROQUETOIRE - MAMETZ and ROQUETOIRE - CRECQUES.

86th. I. Bde. is advancing along road ROQUETOIRE - CRECQUES with an Advance Guard of ½ Battn. and 1 Section R.E.

G.O.C. Brigade - on information received from Cavalry - orders the River to be bridged in 4 places to get the Infantry of Brigade across. Therefore O.C.,510th. Field Coy. sends up his remaining 3 Sections to expedite construction of the Light Bridges.

Pontoon and Trestle Equipment has been used across AIRE - St.OMER Canal, has been taken up - but not yet arrived and therefore not available.

S Banks Keast

Major.R.E.

Date:

O.C. 510th. Field Company R.E.

O.C. No. 1 Section.

You will construct at G.27.d.36.95 (just E. of Mill) a Barrel Raft to transport Field Guns across River. Section with Advance Guard reports Barrels close to above co-ordinates.

(Limber will be taken across River on Raft when completed. After Inspection Raft will be dismantled and timber and barrels disposed of as per instructions from Captain.)

Major.R.E.

Date O.C. 510th. Field Company R.E.

O.C. No. 2 Section.

You are attached to 86th. Brigade Advance Guard. On arrival at Demolished Bridge at G.27.c.68.70. you will make a Rope Bridge somewhere W. of that point.

On completion of above an Endless Rope with tackle for swimming horses across River will be made in same stretch and animals swum across.

Major.R.E.

Date O.C. 510th. Field Company R.E.

O.C. No. 3 Section.

You will make a Single File Barrel Bridge at a suitable point between G.27.c.68.70. and a point 100 yards E. of it. Information received from O.C. Section with Advance Guard that Barrels and Timber found close to stretch in question.

Major.R.E.

Date O.C. 510th. Field Company R.E.

O.C. No. 4 Section.

You will construct 2 Light Trestle Bridges for Infantry in single file at a point just WEST of Saw Mill at G.27.d.30.90.
(The timber for this job is loaned to us by Proprietor of Saw Mill and must not be damaged or cut. Asfew nails as possible will be used. Care must be taken that all timber is returned.)

Major.R.E.

Date O.C. 510th. Field Company R.E.

CONFIDENTIAL

WAR DIARY

OF

510TH (LONDON) FIELD COY. R.E.

VOLUME 26

FROM 1-8-18 TO 31-8-18

Volume 26 - 570th Field Coy RE

WAR DIARY
or
INTELLIGENCE SUMMARY.
(Erase heading not required.)

Army Form C. 2118.

Instructions regarding War Diaries and Intelligence Summaries are contained in F. S. Regs., Part II. and the Staff Manual respectively. Title pages will be prepared in manuscript.

Map Ref S.27 & 36A

Place	Date 1918	Hour	Summary of Events and Information	Remarks and references to Appendices
B 27	Aug 1st		Coy Drill. Officers & Senior NCOs reconnoitred ~~Support~~ Line - Antwerp XV Corps with Officers of 3rd Australian Field Coy.	
	2nd		Coy moved from S.27/R7 a 30.20 to Billets in BORRE. Horse Lines to V 20 b 3.3	
	3rd		No 1 & 3 Sect salvaging RE material - Support Line. No 2 & 4 Sect salvaging RE & other material BORRE. Reconnoitred Right Sub Sector - Reconnoitred Battle Position D LINE. Visited Horse Lines.	Left of Z Line handed over to 9th Divn RE
	4th		No 1, 3 & 4 Sect on Z Line. No 2 Sect Road Repairs. Reconnaissance for Light Line. Forward Dump formed at E.4 b 62.25. Z Line in Left Sector handed over to Kent Field Coy	
	5th		Work as for 4th inst. New Support Line (Actual Line non-existent) taken over from KENTS. Reconnaissance of Right Sector with G.O.C. & B.M. 86th I Bde. Night parties on Breastworks & Drains 150 Infantry	
	6th		Work for 1, 3 & 4 Sects as above. No 2 Sect Camouflaging RE Dump at E.4 b 62.25 & work on Trench D Outs on Z Line. Took OC No 4 Sect over work. He commenced on 7th constructing Strong Points & propping Cellars. Round Z Line with CRE	
	7th		Work 1, 2 & 3 Sects as above. Also No 3 Sect Erection of C Type Shelters at Support Battn HQ. No 4 Sect a) Strengthening Cellars for T.M.B. STRAZEELE STN b) 3 Buildings in E 11 a - Strengthening Cellars & making Defensive Posts of Firing E 11 c 65.75 towards E 11 d 85.85. 2Lt KS DODD to Rouen for RE Course	
	8th		Work as for 7th. Also No 2 Section repairing wire in front of Z Line	

(A7092). Wt. W12839/M1293. 750,000. 1/17. D. D. & L., Ltd. Forms/C.2118/14.

510th Field Coy RE

2

WAR DIARY
or
INTELLIGENCE SUMMARY.

(Erase heading not required.)

Instructions regarding War Diaries and Intelligence Summaries are contained in F. S. Regs., Part II, and the Staff Manual respectively. Title pages will be prepared in manuscript.

Army Form C. 2118.

Place	Date	Hour	Summary of Events and Information	Remarks and references to Appendices
BEF	Aug 1918	→	Work as for 8th inst.	
	9th		Work as for 9th inst. Lt RIDDEL RE joined Coy from RCBD	
	10th	→	Work as for 10th inst.	
	11th		Work as for 11th inst. – Also No 2 Sect. Screening Road E side from E.4.b 62.25 – Northwards	
	12th		Work as for 12th inst. T.M.B. Cellar S. G. Proof at STRAZEELE Stn Completed. Railway	
	13th		Reconnaissance STRAZEELE – HAZEBROUCK by Lt RIDDEL with CRE round work. Road Mines at E 3 d 37 – W 29 c 5.3 & W 19 d 0.6 taken over from W. Ridings.	
	14th		Work as for 13th inst. Inspected Horselines	
	15th		Work as for 14th inst. Also 1st Sect. Started S.Ps at E 6 c 15.30 & E 11 a 4.7.	
	16th	–	Work as for 15th inst. Round Line with G.O.C. 86th I. Bde. To Horselines	
	17th		Work as for 16th. No 2 Sect. started on Charge Boxes for Road Mines & Gas proofing Cellar RAP E 10 b 4.9	
	18th		9th & 29th Divn Attack. – No Work for Company in attack. Rifle from Swift R 1 Coy	
	19th		No 1 Section Z Line & Construction of 3 Man Shelters off same Line	
			No 2 Section a) Recon. of Road Mines b) Screening c) Road Repairs d) Gas Proofing RAP E 10 b 4.9 e) Wire Repairs Z Line	
			No 3 Section Z Line & Const. of 3 Man Shelters off same b) Support Battn HQ Shelter	
			No 4 Section Strong Points. 86th Brigade Attack	
	20th		No 1 Sect. Work on Z Line & Fetching A Frames from B LINE. No 2 Sect. Tracks. No 3 Sect. Work on Z Line	[signature] Major RE
			No 4 Sect. Tracks. No Working Parties. Reconnoitred Captured Ground	

(A7092). Wt. W12839/M1293. 750,000. 1/17. D. D. & L., Ltd. Forms/C.2118/14.

510th Field Coy RE

WAR DIARY
or
~~INTELLIGENCE SUMMARY.~~
(Erase heading not required.)

Instructions regarding War Diaries and Intelligence Summaries are contained in F. S. Regs., Part II. and the Staff Manual respectively. Title pages will be prepared in manuscript.

Army Form C. 2118.

Place	Date Aug 1918	Hour	Summary of Events and Information	Remarks and references to Appendices
B.E.F.	21st		No 1 Section Z Line No Infantry	
			No 2 Section Road Repairs STRAZEELE - VIEUX BERQUINRE W.29.c.58.31 to E.11.c.92.25 - Gas Proofing R.A.P. E.10.b.3.9	
			No 3 Section Z Line No Infy - Shelter Rack ADS BORRE	
			No 4 Road Repairs E.11.c.92.25 towards CELERY COPSE	
	22nd		No 1 Section as for 21st No 3 Sect as for 21st	
			No 2 & 4 Sects & 200 Infantry Road Repts as for 21st. No 4 Sect also on S.P.s & Cellars in E.11.a	
			MOVE No 2 Sect from BORRE to [illegible] E.10.b.3.9	
	23rd		Work as for 22nd. No 4 Section move from BORRE to E.3.d.20.75	
	24th		[illegible] No 1 Sect Work on Z Line - Trench & Shelters - 50 Infy	
			No 2 Sect Road work 150 Infy No 3 Sect Work on Z Line & Wire - 50 Infy - Shelter "C" Type	
			86th Bde HQ - ADS CQMS Store - No 4 Sect Line Battn HQ at E.12.a.8.7 Shelter	
			- S.Ps & Cellars in E.11.a - 1 Platoon Pioneers Lightly - No 2 Sect moved to	
			W.27.d. central	
	25th		HQ moved to E.3.d.20.75 & No 3 Sect to W.27.d. central	
			Work as for 24th except Pioneers not working. Lt. EALDEN RE arrived from 3rd Pontoon Park	
	26th		Work as for 25th	
	27th		" " 26th Only ½ Infantry Parties owing to taking no more front. Lt. RIDDEL to 3rd Pontoon Park	
				[signature] Major RE

510th Field Coy RE

Instructions regarding War Diaries and Intelligence Summaries are contained in F. S. Regs., Part II. and the Staff Manual respectively. Title pages will be prepared in manuscript.

WAR DIARY
or
~~INTELLIGENCE SUMMARY.~~
(Erase heading not required.)

Army Form C. 2118.

Place	Date 1918	Hour	Summary of Events and Information	Remarks and references to Appendices
B.E.F.	August 28th		Part of Left Brigade Front taken over from 497th (Kent) Field Coy: up to line F.10.a.4.3 – E.22.d.8.6.	
			No1 & 3 Sectns L Line No Infantry	
			No2 Sectn of Road Mines – reconstruction of – b) Laying out Mule Track	
			No4 Sectn Battn HQ in E.12.a & Cellars & SP in E.11.a.	
	29th		No1 Sectn L Line – 70 Infantry – No3 Sectn L Line 61 Infantry	
			No2 Sectn Mule Track – 50 Infy – Road Mines – Sown Reconnaissance charges – Removed	
			No4 Sectn 50 Infy Battn HQ & finishing off SP & Cellars	
	30th		Work as for 29th Additional No1 Sectn evening road repair for Guns No2 Sectn (L.N.E.O. line) with 100 Infantry repairs road MERRIS – F.1.a.8.2 Lt MEFFETT	
			EALDEN road reconnaissance in front of OUTTERSTEENE.	
			Dy Mt reconnaissance – Outtersteene	
	31st		Forward Roads Roads made passable for limbers & guns to within a few 100x of Front Posts with Infantry 150 – Pioneers 2 Coy & 4 Sectns Sappers	
			Road reconnaissance forward to close STORK Farm	
			No1 Sectn moved forward to F.8.a.40.85. Line evening LA BECQUE – A.10 Central	

S. Bauld Read Major RE

Copy No 6

MOVEMENT ORDER NO.6.

510th.(London) Field Company. R.E. 22-8-18

Map Ref: Sheet 36A 1:40,000.

1. Nos. 2 ~~& 4~~ Sections will move from present location on 22-8-18 to new billets at ~~E.4.c.3.8. and depots on Railway Sidings at E.4.c.2.6~~. E.10.b.3.9. SBK

~~2. The R.A.P. at E.10.b.39. will not be occupied.~~ Cancelled. SBK

3. Captain will arrange for Section Limbers to be at BORRE at 4 pm. These limbers will return to horselines on completion of move.

4. Nos. 2 ~~& 4~~ Sections Rations will be sent straight to SBK ~~E.4.c.3.8.~~ 10.b.3.9. by the Captain.

5. Move will be completed by 8pm. and completin of move will be reported to Coy.H.Q. by Section Commanders by Code Word "HADID".

S Bankes Read
MAJOR, R.E.
O.C. 510th. (LONDON) FIELD COY. R.E.

Copies to 1. O.C. No 2 Section,
~~2. O.C. No.4 "~~ Cancelled
3. C.R.E.
4. Captain.
5. File.
6. War Diary. ✓

Copy No.8.

510th.Field Coy.R.E.

MOVEMENT ORDER NO.7.

Map Ref:- STRAZEELE 1:20,000. 24-8-18.

1. No.2. Section will move on 24-8-18 from billets at E.10.b.4.9. to billets at W.27.d.central. Move to be completed by 8 pm.
2. Nos.1 & 3 Sections will move on 25-8-18 from present billets at BORRE to billets at W.27.d.central. Move to be completed by 10 am.
3. Coy.H.Q. will move on 25-8-18 from present location at BORRE to farm at E.3.d.20.75. Move to be completed by 10 am.
4. Coy.H.Q. will close at BORRE at 10 am. on 25-8-18 and re-open at E.3.d.20.75 at same hour.
5. Captain will arrange for necessary transport direct with Section Commanders.
6. Completion of move will be reported to Coy.H.Q. at E.3.d.20.75 By Code Word "NAHAS".

[signature]

Major R.E.,

O.C.510th.Field Coy.R.E.

Copies to:-

1. O.C.No.1.Section.
2. " No.2. "
3. " No.3. "
4. " No.4. "
5. Captain.
6. C.R.E.
7. File.
8. War Diary. ✓
9. 86th.Inf.Bde.

Copy No. 8

510th.(London) Field Coy.R.E.

MOVEMENT ORDER NO.8.

Map Ref:- MERRIS, 1:20,000, Edition 2a (local). 31-8-18.

1. No.1 Section will move on evening of 31-8-18 to Bivouac Camp in F.8.c. ,West of road running N.E. & S.W. through square.
   Exact location of Camp to be reported to Coy.Office as early as possible.

2. Nos. 2,3 & 4 Sections and Coy.H.Q. will move to above mentioned Camp on 1-9-18.
   Sections will dump their packs on way to work and return there on completion of work.

3. Sections Transport, Coy.H.Q.Gear, tents and Bivouacs from Horse Lines will be sent up early on morning of 1-9-18 to new Camp. They will return to Horse Lines on completion. Captain will supervise Move which will be completed by 10.30 am.

4. Transport will move forward from present location to W.27.d. central on 1-9-18. Move to be completed by NOON.

5. Coy.H.Q. will close at JOBBERY CROSSING at 9 am. and re-open in F.8.c. at same hour.

6. Completion of move to be reported to Coy.H.Q. by Code Word "SOLB".

[signature]

Major R.E.,
O.C.510th.(London) Field Company R.E.

Copies to:-

1. O.C.No.1 Section,
2. " No.2 "
3. " No.3 "
4. " No.4 "
5. Captain,
6. C.R.E.,
7. File,
8. War Diary, ✓
9. 86th.Inf.Bde.

Vol 27

CONFIDENTIAL.

WAR DIARY

OF

510TH (LONDON) FIELD COY. R.E.

FROM 1-9-1918 TO 30-9-18

VOLUME 27.

Volume 27   510th Field Coy. RE

Instructions regarding War Diaries and Intelligence Summaries are contained in F. S. Regs., Part II. and the Staff Manual respectively. Title pages will be prepared in manuscript.

WAR DIARY
or
INTELLIGENCE SUMMARY.
(Erase heading not required.)

Army Form C. 2118.

Place	Date Sept 1918	Hour	Summary of Events and Information	Remarks and references to Appendices
B.E.7	1.		Company moved from JUBBERY Crossing to OUTTERSTEENE. Transport from HAZEBROUCK to W.27.d. central. All Sections on Forward Road.	
	2		Whole Coy moved to SEENTJE. No 1&4 Sectns on STEENWERCK Bridge & Forward Road. No 3 Sectn Water Supply. No 2 Sect Roads.	
	3		Nos 2&4 Sectns Bridging & Forward Roads. No 3 Sectn Watersupply. No 1 Sect moved to near STEENWERCK STN to make 10 ton Lorry Bridge. Road reconnoitred up to & including NIEPPE	
	4th		No 1 Sect on bridge at STEENWERCK STN: No 2 Sectn Reserve. No 3 Sect. - Forward Roads - Trees cleared at B.15.b. across Main Road. No 4 " " [illegible]. Cleared road B.15.b.5.8 to BRUNE GAYE - unable to get further M.G & Shellfire. Whole Coy moved up to TRABOT.	
	5th		No 1 Sect Bridge at STEENWERCK STN. Completed. No 2 Sect Road Cleared through NIEPPE. No 3 In Reserve. No 4 Detailing new road near Crater at B.8.a.8.7 - Bridge material sent forward - Ponton Equipment checked. Roads in STEENWERCK cleared of fallen trees. Gas shelled at 4 am. 6c Camp.	Water Supply.
	6th		Not possible to get on with Forward Roads. Horsewatering Point with pumps & 40' troughing at B.15.b.0.8 & B.14.a.5.9. - Notice [illegible] the Water Point	
	7th		Forward Road in Progress. Water Point B.13.b.3.6 for 500 animals per hour - 60%	
	8th		Water Point B.13.b.3.6 Complete. Road Surveyed STEENWERCK - B.8.a.8.7 - B.9.c.2.6	

[signature] Major R.E.

Instructions regarding War Diaries and Intelligence Summaries are contained in F. S. Regs., Part II. and the Staff Manual respectively. Title pages will be prepared in manuscript.

WAR DIARY
or
INTELLIGENCE SUMMARY.
(Erase heading not required.)

Army Form C. 2118.

Place	Date Sept 1918	Hour	Summary of Events and Information	Remarks and references to Appendices
AE 7	9		No1 Sect. Filling Craters at B 8 a 8 7 & improving Horse Standings at Watering Pt. No2 Sect. Reserve. No3 Sect. Wattle Boarding Water Point. No4. Repair STEENWERCK - TROIS ARBRES Road. Coy moved from TROIS ARBRES to W. 16 d. 20 15 (CRE Div. No 70 99 15) 2Lt. DODD returned from Rouen.	
	10"		Fixing up Billets etc. at W. 16. d. 20. 15. Orders received to move to HAZEBROUCK (CRE M.O. 71)	
	11		(Movement Order No 9) Moved to HAZEBROUCK 10 a.m. Located V. 22. c. 9. 0. Horse Lines V. 21. b. 6 8.	
	12"		Lectures - Filling Shell Holes. Road Repairs. Checking Equipment & Rations. Iron. Working bayonets. Conference - CRE Coy Commanders & 2nd i/c.	
	13"		Coy Parade - Drill & Gas Measures. Demonstration by CRE - Training of a Section.	
	14"		Coy Parade - Training of Section. Lewis Gun Teams on Range	
	15"		Divl. RE. Church Parade.	
	16"		Company Training 9 am - 12.30 pm on I.G.T. Lines	
	17"		Ditto	
	18		Ditto. Coy moved to ROAD CAMP. S.27/F.25.d.3.3 - Dismounted	
	19"		Company Training. [illegible] by Rail - Mounted by Road	
	20"		At ROAD CAMP. To CRE Conference 5 P.M. Coy moved to WILKINS Camp S/27/F.25.a.2.9.	S Banks Read Maj. RE

A7092). Wt. W128;9/M1297 750,000. 1/17. D. D & L., Ltd. Forms/C2118/14.

Instructions regarding War Diaries and Intelligence Summaries are contained in F. S. Regs., Part II. and the Staff Manual respectively. Title pages will be prepared in manuscript.

WAR DIARY
or
~~INTELLIGENCE~~ ~~SUMMARY~~.
(Erase heading not required.)

Army Form C. 2118.

Place	Date Sept. 1918	Hour	Summary of Events and Information	Remarks and references to Appendices
B.27	21st		Company Parade – Gas instruction & prolonged wearing of masks.	
	22nd		Company moved from S27/F.25.a.2.9 to ORILLIA Camp B.26c.6.2. Sheet 28 N.W. & Transport to A.29.d central. Morning work on Discs for Burial Officer.	
	23rd		Company work on Discs. S. Capt & ... with CRE at Dump. CRE's Conference 3pm. Writing Op. orders. No.1 Sect. work on Goldfish Chateau. Other Sects on Discs etc.	
	24th		No.1 Sect. Goldfish Chateau. No.2 Sect. on Gunner Lines. No.3 Discs & Notice Bds. No.4 Sect. at ORILLIA Dump. Op. & Ad. Instns writing.	
	25th		No.1 Sect. Goldfish Chateau Gasproofing etc. No.2 Sect. Salving timber. No.3 Sect. Notice Boards & WARRINGTON Road Maintenance. No.4 Sect. ORILLIA Dump. Court of Inquiry held on Lost Cycle & broken denture. No.1 Sect. work at Goldfish Chateau. Coy:	
	26th		Company Parade 8.30am Gas Inst. Conference 10am–12 noon.	
	27th		Light work. No.4 Sect. B.3 Bridges – School Road & Lille Gate Rd – Making up on tramway. No.3 Sect. making up Warrington Rd for W. end School Road – Notice Boarding. 2 Drivers wounded. 1 Horse killed – Pontoon Wagon Damaged. Fieldguns to front line	
	28th		Operation. Attack by 29th Divn. No.1 Sect. Preparing for Field guns – ZILLEBEKE – HELL FIRE CORNER Road & LEINSTER Rd. – No.2 Section – Warrington Rd from Front Line forward & Ext. to Halfway House. Very Successful Day.	[illegible signature]

Instructions regarding War Diaries and Intelligence Summaries are contained in F. S. Regs., Part II. and the Staff Manual respectively. Title pages will be prepared in manuscript.

WAR DIARY
or
INTELLIGENCE SUMMARY.
(Erase heading not required.)

Army Form C. 2118.

Place	Date Sept 1917	Hour	Summary of Events and Information	Remarks and references to Appendices
I.2.7	29		Work on Plank Road HOOGE to JARGON CROSS Roads	
			1. Sect. by night } 2 Sections by day.	
			1. Sect. early morning }	
			No 4 Sect. moved to CLAPHAM JTN. - Rest of Coy. to CHATEAU WOOD	
	30		Work during afternoon on CLAPHAM JTN - MENIN Rd. Whole Coy. moved to J.29.d.	

S Rawlinson Kemp Major RE

(A7092). Wt. W12839/M1293. 750,000. 1/17. D. D. & L., Ltd. Forms/C.2118/14.

54th Field Company R.E.

Movement Order No. 10.

Map Ref. Sheet 27 1/40000 — Dated 19/9/17.

28 N.W. 1/20000

5A Hazebrouck 1/40000

1. The Coy will move with 56th Infy Bde Group from present area to II Corps area on 19th inst.

2. Dismounted Personnel will move by train entraining at HONDEGHEM STN METRE GAUGE V.2.d.4.6 & detraining at POPERINGHE. (See Table attached)

3. Coy Transport under Lt EALDEN will move under 56th Brigade Transport Officer. (See Table attached)

4. Lt MERRETT & 1 N.C.O. & 1 Sapper will report to 56th Infy Bde H.Q. at 2 p.m. & will travel on Divnl. Bus Lorry as Advance Party.

Advance Parties will report to Staff Capt at A.P.M. at rendezvous in new Billeting Area. The Rendezvous will be notified to Advanced Parties at 2 P.M. at Bde HQ.

Billeting Officer will meet dismounted Personnel at POPERINGHE STN at 23.25 hrs 19/9/17 & guide them to new Camp.

5. Capt GODFREY R.E. will be entraining Officer for the Unit & will report to Entrainment Officer (Capt C. St. L. WEBB / R.I.F.) at HONDEGHEM at 19.30 hrs.

6. Rations for consumption on 20th inst will proceed Loaded on Supply Wagons with transport of Unit. Supply Wagons will rejoin 2 Coy A.S.C. on 20th inst.

7. Present Billets will be handed over to Town Major by 2nd Lt COATES by 6 P.M. obtaining Certificate to the effect that they have been left clean. Not

all furniture etc taken over - as per inventory in Coy. Office - has been handed over.

M. CHARTON Interpreter will make out billeting Certificate in accordance with instructions issued by Brigade Interpreter.

8. All Personnel due for leave on 22nd inst & onwards will proceed with Units to new Area

9. DISMOUNTED PERSONNEL

Sections will Parade at 6.45 PM in Marching Order outside Billets. Caps will be worn. Unconsumed portion of days ration & filled water bottles will be carried.

Blankets & L. Guns will be carried on Sect. Transport.

1. Cook per Sect. will accompany dismounted personnel with. Dixie & material for making tea. The other Sect. Cook will brake Sect. Limber.

Head of Column will pass Starting Point (S27/ V. 22 C.2.7 Cross Roads) at 7.25 p.m. behind 2/R.Fs & will arrive at HONDEGHEM STN. at 8.10. P.M. Coy. will entrain on TRAIN No. IV. which will depart at 20-47 Hrs & arrive at POPERINGHE at 23-25 Hours.

10. MOUNTED PERSONNEL & Brakesmen.

STARTING POINT Cross Roads V.22.a.9.0. Sheet 27. Time head of Coy Transport will pass STARTING POINT 8.15 P.M. They will march behind Bde HQ & T.M.B.

25 Yards will be maintained between every group

3

of 6 Vehicles & 100x between transport of each Unit.

ROUTE:- STEENVOORDE - ABEELE (27/L.26.c) - POPERINGHE - NORTH SWITCH ROAD - Cross Roads A.25.d. - Cross Roads A 30 central. From latter point transport will be met & guided to Coy Camp.

Div. Marching Order - Off Caps.

Lt EALDEN will issue his own orders for time of parade & will arrange to have Sect Lumbers - Limbers - Mess Cart & Office gear etc loaded before 6.P.M.

11. All H. QF & Sect Kit - Blankets &c must be ready for loading by 5 P.M.

12. Cyclists under Senior Cyclist N.C.O. will move off at 8.P.M. & proceed to POPERINGHE RLY STN. - via STEENVORDE & ABEELE & await arrival of Coy at that point.

Issued at 12.35 PM
19.9.16.

[signature]
MAJOR, R.E.
O.C. 510th. (LONDON) FIELD COY R.E.

510th FIELD COY R.E.

Movement Order No 11.

Map Ref. Sheet 27 1/40000 Dated 21/9/18

Sheet 28 NW 1/20000

1.) The Coy: will move tomorrow as follows

a) DISMOUNTED PORTION by TRAIN to ORILLIA CAMP S.25/H.2.a.7.9. TRAIN arrangement to be notified later (About 6 P.M.)

b) MOUNTED PORTION by Road March commencing at 7.30 P.M to Horse Lines at S.25/A.2 9 d. Central

2.) A Billeting Party consisting of II Lt COATES & all Cyclists (except 2 Coy Runners who will go by train with cycles) will report to O.C. Billets: at ORILLIA CAMP at 6 P.M. – who will arrange accommodation

3.) Capt: Godfrey R.E. will supervise move by Train & Lt EARDEN R.E. move of transport by Road.

4. All men will wear Marching Order – S.D. Kit, Slung & Soft Caps. Haversack Ration to be carried.

5.) Details for transport of Section Blankets, Cooking Gear & Officers Baggage ~~thereof~~ will be notified later.

6.) Capt Godfrey & Lt EARDEN will obtain a "CLEAN CAMP LINES" certificate from Camp Warden.

7.) Time of Parade for Dismounted Personnel will be ordered by Capt Godfrey & for mounted by Lt EARDEN of later.

Issued at 10.45 am. [illegible]

22/4/18. Maj. R.E.

List of Material at Dumps.

on evening of 22-9-18.

Dump Location.	Material.	
I.15.c.6.6.	Shovels	100
	Baby Elephant	1
	Hurdles	20
	Pickets, wood, long	40
	" " short	20
	Wire, plain, coil	1
I.15.c.9.6.	Picks	5
	Shovels	30
I.15.d.0.7.	Shovels	20
I.15.b.6.5.	Hurdles	30
	Pickets, wood, long	60
	" " short	30
	Wire, plain, coils	2
St. PIERRE I.8.c.8.0.	Hurdles	150
	X.P.M. Frames	50
	Trench boards	90
	Pickets, wood, 6'	350
	" " 3'	150
	A Frames	74
	Wire, plain, coils	20
	" barbed, coils	30
	" concertina, coils	50
	Picks	170
	Shovels	100
	Mauls	4
	Cement, barrels	1
LILLE GATE I.14.a.5.2.	Artillery Bridges	3
	Sandbags	250
	1 Train load of road slabs to be delivered shortly.	
I.13.c.7.2. H.18.d.9.5. KRUISTRAAT	Beech Slabs	400
	6" Spikes, cwts	~~8~~ 5
	6" Nails	2
	Sandbags	5000
	14 lb. Hammers	12
	Shovels	50
	Picks	25
	Felling Axes	10
	Hand Axes	10
	Wire Cutters	40
	3' Cross Cuts	4
	Wheelbarrows	20
	Mauls	8
	3lb. Hammers	12
	Scoops or Buckets	20
	Adzes	2
HELL FIRE CORNER	Road Metal	
HOW SPUR I.15.a.5.1.	Reserve of 50 Beech Slabs.	

SECRET. | 510th. Field Company R.E. | Copy No. 6

OPERATION ORDER No. 3.

Map Refs. Sheet 28 N.W.4 1:10,000 | Dated 23-9-18.

28 N.E.3 1:10,000

1. The 29th. Division will attack on a date and at an hour to be notified later, in conjunction with 35th. Divn. of ~~10~~ 19th. Corps on its right and 9th. Divn. of 2nd. Corps on its left.

2. Boundaries and Objectives.

Boundaries. N.Divl. Boundary I.7.d.0.6. - I.8.c.60.35. - I.9.c.7.6. - HELL FIRE CORNER - JARGON CROSS ROADS.

S.Divl. Boundary I.20.a.6.9. - I.21.b.0.8. - I.22.b.35.10. - I.22.b.80.05. - I.24.b.9.5.

East of last points given for N. and S.Boundaries Divl. Boundaries will run approx. 1000 yards N. and S. of MENIN Road and parallell to same.

Objectives.

86th. and 87th. Brigades will probably take up to the line J.~~14.a.~~ 19.b. central - ~~CLAPHAM JTN.~~ TO - ~~I.24.b.9.5.~~ J.9.d.8.6. and if all goes well 88th. Brigade will push on beyond this on new alignment.

3. The 29th. Division will attack on a two Brigade front, 87th. Infantry Brigade on right and 86th. Infantry Brigade on left.

4. The Company is allotted the following tasks :-

on I/J NIGHT.

(a) Repair of WARRINGTON Road for Field Artillery from I.20.a.65.85. to FRONT LINE I.15.d.9.4.

(b) Remove Dummy Block LILLE GATE.

(c) Fix bridge over trench at I.14.c.75.86.

(d) Fix bridges over trenches in SCHOOL ROAD at I.15.a.9.6. and I.15.b.05.85. and repair shell holes.

On J DAY.

(a) Open up WARRINGTON Road from FRONT LINE to I.16.d.6.5. for Field Guns.

(b) Open up for Field Guns Road from I.16.d.6.5. to HELL FIRE CORNER.

(c) Open up for Field Guns Road from ~~I.16.b.05.43.~~ I.10.c.90.05. to MENIN Road at ~~I.10.d.75.07.~~ I.10.d.15.15.

(d) When a, b and c completed take over from ~~455th.~~ 497th. Field Coy. repair of Road ~~I.16.d.60.45. to LEINSTER Road I.17.c.7.6. to~~ BIRR CROSS ROADS to HALF WAY HOUSE I.17.c.8.7.

(e) ALL NOTICE BOARD~~S~~ING up to and including HELL FIRE CORNER - ZILLEBEKE Road.

On J + 1 Day.

Work on this day will depend on the success of the attack and if all goes well will probably consist of opening up MENIN Road to HOOGE - thence by Northern Deviation (Track B) as far as JARGON CROSS Roads J.7.d.9.2. to road junction J.14.a.45.55. to MENIN Road at CLAPHAM JUNCTION - thence along MENIN Road.

5. Work is allotted as follows :-

On I/J NIGHT.

No.3 Section. Repair of WARRINGTON Road for Field Artillery from I.20.c.65.85. to present FRONT LINE I.15.d.9.4. Only a single track will be concentrated on. Second i/c will detail 1 G.S. and 3 Pontoon Wagons under a Mounted N.C.O. to work under O.C. No.3 Section to draw slabs and spikes etc. at KRUISTRAAT Dump and feed Sappers laying slabs.

These notice boards will be bundled and taken on Pack animal and strongly erected at place shown.

(h) Patrol and repair if necessary WARRINGTON Road between KRUISTRAAT and I.20.a.6.8.

(i) Tools as laid down for No. 3 Section will be carried.

6. J DAY.

No.2 Section.

(a) Open up WARRINGTON Road from FRONT LINE to I.16.d.6.5. for Field Guns. Probable number of slabs required about 100. Second i/c will detail 3 Pontoon and 1 G.S. Wagon with Mounted N.C.O. to work under O.C. No. 2 Section for the work. O.C. No. 2 Section will provide loading party at KRUISTRAAT Dump.

A forward party should be provided to clear away debris from sections of slab road to be repaired and prepare for new slabs - followed by a second party who will unload slabs from wagons, lay loosely and proceed forward with wagons laying slabs direct off wagons as they go. A third party will spike down.

(b) Erect following NOTICE BOARDS :-

MOATED GRANGE
I.16.c.6.7.

WARRINGTON Road 2 Boards erect at I.16.c.65.35.

and I.16.d.58.55.

I.16.d.58.55. E.end WARRINGTON Rd.

← HELL FIRE CORNER	
ZILLEBEKE →	

Erect opposite E. end of WARRINGTON Rd.

(c) On completion of a and b men will be moved forward and work on Road ~~I.16.c.60.45~~. - I.17.c.~~7.6~~ 8.7. to BIRR CROSS ROADS ~~to~~ taking work on this road over from ~~assist West Riding and~~ Kent Field Company~~s~~. ~~Special attention will be devoted to the road round HALF WAY HOUSE which is very bad.~~

Slabs may be removed from LNINSTER Road south of the point I.17.c.7.5. for above work.

Tools as laid down for No. 3 Section will be carried.

14 lb. hammers will be drawn from KRUISTRAAT Dump. Slabs, spikes and sandbags will be available at that Dump.

In the event of 20th A.T. Coy. R.E. arriving to take over WARRINGTON ROAD before it has been completed by No 2 Section O.C. No 2 Section will immediately hand over WARRINGTON ROAD up to I.16.d.6.5. to O.C. 20th A.T. Coy. R.E. & push forward & work on LEINSTER ROAD I.17.c.8.7. northwards as laid down in (c) above.

No.1 Section.

(a) Open up for Field Guns Road from I.16.d.6.5. to HELL FIRE CORNER.(Metalled Road and as road stone is not likely to be available - plenty of sandbags should be carried.

(b) Ditto. Road from ~~I.16.b.05.43~~ I.10.c.95.05. to MENIN Road at ~~I.10.d.73.07~~ I.10.d.15.15.

(c) Erect following NOTICE BOARDS :-

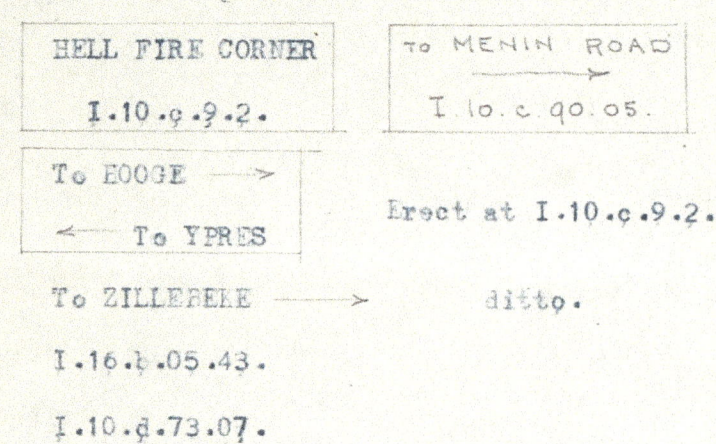

HELL FIRE CORNER I.10.c.9.2.	TO MENIN ROAD → I.10.c.90.05.

To HOOGE → ← To YPRES	Erect at I.10.c.9.2.
To ZILLEBEKE →	ditto.

I.16.b.05.43.

I.10.d.73.07.

Pack Animals should be used for carriage of sandbags, notice boards, tools etc.

( ) On completion of a, b and c the Section will be pushed forward

No.3 Section will provide the loading party at KRUISTRAAT - ~~not more than~~ about 1 N.C.O. + 4 men - and unloading will be done by the Sappers working on the Road.

About 270 slabs necessary.

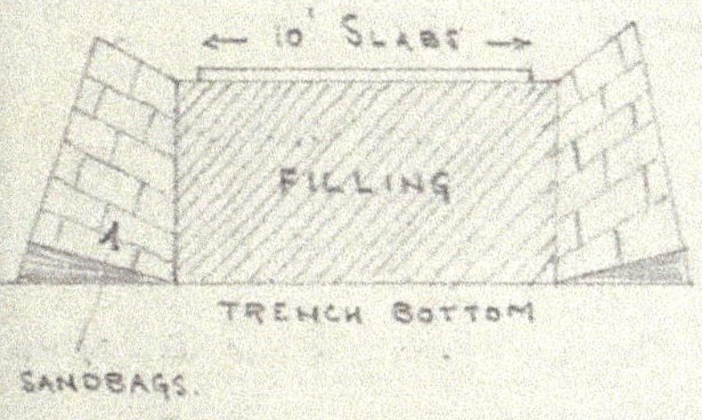

The Trench crossings at I.15.c.35.35.- I.15.c.95.60 and I.15.d.9.4. will be filled in. Strong Sandbag Revetments being built on each side of road from bottom of trench and filled in between and slabbed surface laid. (see sketch.)

All slabs will be rapidly laid - loose first to allow wagons to move forwardand deposit slabs where required. A party will be detailed to clear away broken slabs and prepare sections to be repaired for new slabs. A rear party spiking down.

All parties must be carefully instructed in their jobs beforehand.

The following tools will be carried : -

2 Light crow bars	2 Felling axes
2 Hand axes	2 Saws
1 Cross cut saw	2 6' Rods
4 Shovels	1 Pick
3 Tracing tapes	1 Maul
3~~4~~ 14 lb. Hammers	3 3lb. Hammers
12 Wire Cutters	1 Adze

14 lb. hammers will be required for driving spikes. All tools will be drawn from ~~and these will be delivered beforehand to~~ KRUISTRAAT Dump + will be retained by the Section during operations ~~- these will be returned to the Dump on completion of work.~~

Only the Section will be available for this work.

No.4 Section.

(a) Remove Dummy Block at LILLE GATE.

(b) Fix Bridge at I.14.c.75.86. Bridge is on site.

(c) Fix Bridges over trenches on SCHOOL Road at I.15.a.9.6. and I.15.b.05.85. Bridges and spikes on sites.

(d) Make up over Light Tramway at junction SCHOOL Road and LILLE GATE - SHRAPNEL CORNER Road.

(e) Fill shell holes in SCHOOL Road and ROad from LILLE GATE - WARRINGTON Road.

(f) Clear knife rests off road at about I.14.c.75.38.

(g) Erect following NOTICE BOARDS :-

SCHOOL ROAD	4 Boards at	I.14.c.77.80. I.15.a.30.18. I. 9.d.45.15. I. 9.d.45.45.
WARRINGTON ROAD	4 Boards at	I.14.c. 9. 1. I.20.a.65.87. (2 boards one each side of road) I.15.c.65.52.
ZILLEBEKE	Erect where stream crosses WARRINGTON Road.	
I.13.c.35.90.	West End WARRINGTON Road.	
I.13.d.95.08.	Railway Crossing.	
I.20.a.62.88.	Junctn. WARRINGTON Road and LILLE GATE - TROIS ROIS Road.	
I.14.c.76.79.	W. end SCHOOL Road.	
I.15.a.38.22.	SCHOOL Road.	
I. 9.d.43.45.	Jtn. SCHOOL rd. - MENIN Rd.	
← YPRES HOOGE →	Jtn. SCHOOL Rd. - MENIN Rd.	

along MENIN Road and ~~[illegible]~~ takes over from Kent Field Coy. work on Road between I.11.d.4.3. to I.17.c.7.6.

(e) Tools as laid down for No. 3 Section will be carried.

GENERAL.

(a) All N.C.Os. and as many men as possible will carry wire cutters. Every man will carry 10 sandbags tucked into his belt.

(b) All will be in fighting order with 1 days preserved ration and iron rations and filled water bottles.

(c) All Section Commanders - after starting their men at work will reconnoitre the roads allotted to them and send back a report to Coy. Report Centre - showing on Map - the Road or Roads referred to and on back of map - or in separate report - time required to complete tasks also if any extra stores required with quantities of same.

(d) Each Section Commander will be issued with 2 Copies of map 1:10,000 HOOGE.

These will be used for sending back information obtained during operations. Reports will be attached to the maps or written on the back, and actual portions of roads, tracks, tramline etc. reported on, should be distinctly marked on the map.

(e) Section Commanders will make as much use of the Pack Transport + limbers as possible.

(f) Second in Command will be indented on for transport for Operations.

(g) "B" Teams will be formed amongst N.C.Os.

A Section Commander will take out with him his 2nd., 4th., and 6th. senior N.C.O. - leaving Sect. Sergt. and 3rd. and 5th. N.C.Os. as "B" Team.

(h) List of R.E.Dumps and material therein is attached.

(i) Notes circulated to Officers - "Points to be borne in mind during an advance" - will not be lost sight of.

(j) Coy. H. Qrs. will be at H.12.a.6.4.

Coy.Report Centre at LILLE GATE DUG-OUTS - H.Qrs. of W. Riding Field Coy. All reports will be sent to this Location. Corpl. LEE will be at this centre to receive reports.

C.R.E. at GOLDFISH CHATEAU H.11a.8.2.

(k) Captain will form nightly advanced dumps as far forward as possible and on roads which the Coy. is working on. - the dumps to contain material required for next days work.

(l) G.S. and Pontoon Wagons should carry from 20 to 25 slabs for a lengthy trip and 25 to 30 on a short trip over good roads.

(m) Captain will detail 1 G.S. and 3 Pontoon Wagons under Mounted N.C.O. for work under C.R.E. on J + 1 Day. Location to report to and time to be notified later.

(n) Tool Cart equipment will not be used until instructions to do so are issued. Tools &c will be drawn from KRUISTRAAT Dump.

S Bankshead Major R.E.

Issued at O.C.510th.Field Coy. R.E.

Copies to :- 1 O.C.No.1 Section 5 C.R.E.

2 " 2 " 6 War Diary

3 " 3 " 7 File

4 " 4 " 8 Captain

SECRET. | 510th.Field Company R.E. | Copy No. 6.

ADMINISTRATIVE INSTRUCTIONS No. 3.

Map Refs. Sheet 28 N.W.4 1:10,000
28 N.E.3 1:10,000

Dated 24-9-18

(1) SUPPLIES

Every man will carry filled water bottle - which must be sparingly used - 1 days preserved ration and IRON RATION.

(2) S.A.A.

Every man will carry 50 rounds S.A.A.
Reserve Dumps are formed at :-
I. 9.d.4.5. I.10.c.3.4.
I.15.b.4.2.
I. 9.d.2.0.

(3) WATER.

33 Extra Water Bottles are available for the Coy. and 60 Petrol Tins. Section Commanders will arrange with Second i/c for supply from these if they consider necessary.
NO WATER will be DRUNK from shell holes or enemy supplies.

(4) YUKON PACKS

Ten packs are available and may be indented for from Second i/c when required.

(5) SIGNAL ARRANGEMENTS.

Telephone and Telegraph.
Advanced Divl. Exchange - YPRES RAMPARTS.
Exchanges on Buried Routes at :-
I.16.a.5.8. and I.15.c.5.7.
Visual Stations at:-
I.16.b.0.4.
J. 7.c.6.6.
J.14. c.1.7.
These Stations will move forward with Battns.
Wireless.
1 Loop Set and 1 Trench Set with each Brigade H.Q.
D.R.L.S.
Motor Cyclists will work at first up to YPRES RAMPARTS and later up to HELL FIRE CORNER.
510th.Field Coy.R.E.
Report Centre at LILLE GATE DUG-OUTS. All reports will be handed in to Corpl. LEE at this centre.

(6) MEDICAL ARRANGEMENTS.

R.A.Ps. I. 8.d.1.5. St.JACQUES.
I.14.b.2.8. St.PIERRE.

A.D.S. PRISON YPRES I.7.b.2.2.

Corps Walking Wounded Station. H.1.b.7.1.
(TAVISTOCK HOUSE)

Embussing Point for Walking Wounded I.7.c.6.7.

Main Dressing Station H.8.c.6.9.

Following Posts will be formed as early as possible:-

CAR LOADING POSTS	I.17.a.9.7. and I.17.c.4.4.
BEARER RELAY POSTS	I.18.c.4.6.
	J.13.a.1.3.(E.edge of Crater)
	I.23.b.6.8. YEOMANRY POST
	I.24.a.2.4. CROSS ROADS
	J.13.d.6.9. CLAPHAM JTN.

(7) PRISONERS of WAR CAGE. H.4.d.2.8. WINDWARD HOUSE.

(8) R.E.STORES. List of material available is attached to OPERATION ORDER No.3.

(9) FORWARD ACCOMMODATION. In the event of a Section having to remain forward - Buildings and Dug-outs in evacuated area will not be used, but Bivouacs will be provided by Second i/c on demand.

S Banks Keast

Major R.E.
O.C.510th.Field Coy.R.E.

Issued at

Copies to :- 1 to O.C. No.1 Section.
2 " 2 "
3 " 3 "
4 " 4 "
5 C.R.E.
6 War Diary.
7 File.
8 Captain

SECRET. 510th.Field Coy.R.E. Copy No. 6

ADDENDUM to ADMININTRATIVE ORDER No.3.

(1) SUPPLIES

(a) Rations for consumption on J+1 and succeeding days will be delivered by Divl. Train to Transport Lines. On arrival of Train Wagon the rations will be sorted and arranged as required by Units C.Q.M.S. as expeditiously as possible. Train Wagons will wait and as many as are required will convey the rations to Unit Pack Lines. The Unit is responsible that there is a man at their Transport Lines who can guide the Train Wagon to Pack Lines.

(b) Rations are to be delivered early on I DAY for consumption on J DAY, sufficient hard rations being issued to allow all troops going into action to carry one hard ration for consumption on J DAY in addition to their IRON RATIONS.

(c) A full rum ration will be issued early on I DAY for consumption on I-J NIGHT.

(2) SHELTERS.

Following shelters will be drawn any time after 24th. inst. from AREA COMMANDANT - DIRTY BUCKET (S.28/A.30.c.9.9 and taken on charge of Unit :-8 SHELTERS.

These are available for Sections who may have to bivouac forward and will be indented for on 2nd.i/c. as required.

(3) STRAGGLER POSTS and P. of W. CAGE.

(a) First Phase.		S.28./H.3.c.3.5.
		H.3.d.2.3.
		H.9.a.8.7.
	Collecting Station	H.4.d.2.8.
(b) Second Phase.		S.28./I. 7.c.4.7.
		I.13.a.7.4.
		I.13.c.5.9.
	Collecting Post	The Barracks YPRES.
	P. of W. Cage	ditto.

(4) WATERPROOF RATION BAGS.

Waterproof ration bags each holding 50 rations are available and held by Captain for sending Coys. rations forward.

(5) CHAIN of COMMUNICATION.

Section Runners	to	Coy.Report Centre LILLE GATE Dug-outs. I.14.a.95.25.
Coy.Report Centre Col.LEE in charge Runners Spr.DIXON " MORRIS with Cycles.	to	Coy.H.Qrs. MACHINE GUN SIDINGS H.12.a.6.4.

Coy.H.Qrs.		C.R.E.
Capt.GODFREY.	to	Horse Lines.
Runners :-		
2 Mounted.		

[signature]

Copies to all recipients of
ADMINISTRATIVE ORDER No.3.

Major R.E.
O.C.510th.Field Coy.R.E.

SECRET. 510th.Field Company R.E. Copy No. 6

ADDENDUM to OPERATION ORDER No. 3. Date 26-9-18.

(1) Wagons going forward will do so with an interval of 200 yards between pairs of wagons.

(2) Following routes forward will be available :-

(a) POPERINGHE - YPRES Road to MENIN Gate - MENIN Road to HOOGE.

(b) H.12.d.3.4. to KRUISSTRAAT - I.14.c.8.8. - SCHOOL Road - MENIN Road - HOOGE.

(c) H.12.d.3.4. to KRUISSTRAAT - WARRINGTON Road to I.16.d.5.5. to HELL FIRE CORNER.

(d) H.12.d.3.4. through YPRES - LILLE GATE - SCHOOL Road - MENIN Road - HOOGE.

(3) O.C.No.3 Section when finished with 1 G.S.and 3 Pontoon Wagons on I-J NIGHT will see that the Wagons return to KRUISSTRAAT and are loaded up with slabs by his loading party, the Wagons being left at the Dump under charge of Storekeeper until O.C.No.2 Section arrives and takes them over. Teams used on I-J NIGHT will return to Horse-lines on completion of work and Captain will arrange for new teams for J DAY.

(4) All animals will carry double feeds and watering buckets.

(5) Drivers with pack animals will be in fighting order and carry same rations as the Sappers.

(6) Locations :-

86th., 87th., 88th.Infy.Brigades -	RAMPARTS,YPRES	I.14.b.2.9.
H.Q.,Pioneers	LILLE GATE.	I.14.a.95.25.
H.Q.,West Riding Field Coy.	"	"
H.Q.,Kent Field Coy.	INF.BARRACKS.	I.7.d.75.15.
T.M.B.,R.A.	"	I.7.d.9.2.

(7) On J DAY theSecond i/c will be stationed at Coy. H.Qrs. MACHINE GUN SIDINGS. Any stores urgently required,food, water, bivouacs, extra pack animals or limbers will be indented for on him. Full particulars of what is required, when and where required,must be given and a guide provided if necessary.

(8) Slabs should be available on J DAY + about 6 Hours at HELL FIRE CORNER.

S Banks Read

Major R.E.
O.C.510th.Field Coy.R.E.

Copies to all recipients
of OPERATION ORDER No.3.

57th Field Company. R.E.

Movement Order No. 12.

Map Ref. S.28. 1:20000. Dated 26.9.18

1) The Coy. will move to Dugouts at MACHINE GUN SIDINGS - H.12.a.5.4 - less Certain transport - on 27th inst.

2). Captain will arrange for G.S. & 3 Pontoon Wagons & Tool Carts of Nos 3 & 4 Sectns to report at ORILLIA CAMP at 4.P.M. Tool Carts will remain at H.12.a.5.4 & teams return to Horse Lines. Pontoon Wagons & G.S. will proceed forward with No 3 Section for night work.

No 3 & 4 Sectns will dump their Pack Kit etc. at H.12.a.5.4 - leaving same i/c of Cooks & Tool cart men & proceed to work.

3. Tool Carts of Nos 1 & 2 Sectns will report at ORILLIA Camp at 5.45 P.M. with Tool Cart men.

4. Nos 1 & 2 Sectns & H.Qrs dismounted. will proceed to H.12.a.5.4 by Light Railway leaving ORILLIA Camp at 6.30

P.M. Parade with all Kit 6.00 P.M.

5.) All Ranks – except those going on night work who will be in Battle Order, with packs & blankets on wagons – will wear Marching Order – Tin Hats & S.B.Rs at Alert position.

6.) Mounted Personnel will be prepared to move forward to MACHINE GUN Sidings on 28th inst.

7.) Lt MEFFET will show the Cooks etc. of No. 3+4 Sects on arrival at H.12.a.5.4 the billets to be taken over by the Coy. & they will be responsible for billets until rest of Coy. arrive.

[illegible initials]

[illegible initials]

Issued at 8.10. p.m.
26.9.18.

S. Bankhead
Major RE

[illegible initials]

CONFIDENTIAL

WAR DIARY.

OF

510TH (LONDON) FIELD COY. R.E.

VOLUME: 28

FROM: 1-10-18 TO 31-10-18.

V8.28

Volume 28. 570th Field Coy. R.E.

Instructions regarding War Diaries and Intelligence Summaries are contained in F. S. Regs., Part II. and the Staff Manual respectively. Title pages will be prepared in manuscript.

WAR DIARY
or
~~INTELLIGENCE SUMMARY.~~
(Erase heading not required.)

Army Form C. 2118.

Place	Date Oct 1918	Hour	Summary of Events and Information	Remarks and references to Appendices
B.E.F.	1.		No 1 Sect. Work on Div. H.Q. Dug-Outs No 2 & 3 Road Wk between J. 29. b - K. 31. a. No 4 Sect. CRE's Mess.	
	2.		No 1 Sect. Div. H.Q. Dugouts & Mess No 3 & 4 In relief on Road J. 21. b. 4.1 to J. 21. d. 8.9. No 2 Sect. 10 Men on Div! Dump loading Stores	
	3		Work on MENIN Road - all Sectns in 2 Reliefs. Coy. moved during afternoon to CHATEAU WOOD	
	4		Work on clearing Out Dug Outs & making Shelters WESTHOEK for R.E. H.Q.	
	5		No 2 Section moved at 0600 to BECELAERE to construct Advanced DHQ at K 7 c 30.85 (Map 28) 5 Wagon loads Stores sent up. Other Sections cleaning wagons etc.	
	6.		Drew Bridging Equipment from 7 Ponton Park & dumped at J. 12. a. Visited No 2 Section. Lt MEFFET reconnoitred Site for new Camp at K. 1. d. 7.5.	
	7		Coy: moved to K. 1. d. 7.5. Sappers started work at 12.00 Hrs on Adv. DHQ & DAHQ	
	8		No 1 Sect. on Office for D.A.H.Q. & Mess for CRE No 2 Sect. Adv. DHQ No 3 Sect. Road Reps. No 4 Sect. on H.Q. 86th Inf. Bde.	
	9		Work on Adv DHQ D.A.H.Q. CRE H.Q. - Road Screening - Road Reps. 86th & 88th Bde H.Q.	S. Beattie Ke[illegible] Major R.E.

A7092). Wt. W12839/M1293 750,000. 1/17. D. D & L., Ltd. Forms/C2118/14.

Instructions regarding War Diaries and Intelligence Summaries are contained in F. S. Regs., Part II. and the Staff Manual respectively. Title pages will be prepared in manuscript.

WAR DIARY
or
~~INTELLIGENCE SUMMARY.~~
(Erase heading not required.)

Army Form C. 2118.

Place	Date Oct 1918	Hour	Summary of Events and Information	Remarks and references to Appendices
B E F	10		As for 9th with following exception 86th Bde HQ Completed – 4 Infy Bridges Made	
	11		As for 10th except 88th Bde HQ handed over to [illegible] Field Coy. Additional work	
			Deviation track toward K 5 a 1 0 made + Boundary Boards erected	
	12		DAHQ – Adv DHQ + RE HQ Completed – Road Screening 95% Completed.	
			Deviation track toward K 5 a 1 0 made + Bridges Infy over HEULE BEEK erected	
	13		Screening Completed – + DHQ Adv Completed. Lt. HINGÉ joined Company.	
	14th		29th Divn: Attacked. 1 Sectn with B Battery RHA. 2 Sectns ready for [illegible] work	
			Water supply – + Notice Boarding in occupied territory – Reconnaissance	
	15th		Reconnaissance. Water Supply + Notice Boarding	
	16		Ditto Roads + in CUERNE for Bridging material – Water Supply + Notice Boarding	
	17		Ditto	
	18th		Lt Barker Benson went on Leave	
			Bridge Site Reconnaissance by night with Lt Coates.	
	19th		~~Ag~~ MAJOR KEAST DAQ.RE as A/CRE CAPT. GODFREY as A/O.C. 29th Div. forced	
			passage of LYS. 1 Section + 2 Section on barrel pier ferries, + both in conjunction on	

(A9175) Wt W2358/P56 600,000 12/17 D. D. & L. Sch. 52a. Forms/C2118/15.

Instructions regarding War Diaries and Intelligence Summaries are contained in F. S. Regs., Part II, and the Staff Manual respectively. Title pages will be prepared in manuscript.

WAR DIARY
or
~~INTELLIGENCE SUMMARY.~~
(Erase heading not required.)

Army Form C. 2118.

Place	Date Oct 1918	Hour	Summary of Events and Information	Remarks and references to Appendices
B.E.F.				
	19th		floating infantry bridge in H.16.c. 4 Section on field gun bridge at H.11.c.7.5. ½ Coy. Pioneers attached, & 5 G.S. Wagons from Train. Coy. moved to HEULE DUMP (29 N.W. G.12.c.2.1.)	
	20th		Artillery bridge H.11.c.7.5 – No 1 & 2 sections relieved No 4 at 1500, and continued bridge, completing at 2400. Coy. moved to CUERNE.	
	21st		Coy. moved to Fm Van der PUTTE. I.20.c 4.5. Reconnaissance. 2 Section on upkeep of bridge H.11.c.7.5. 4 Section on reconnoitring R.E. dump I.20.c.6.2. & notice-boarding	
	22nd		2 Section storing German float-bridge, & erecting two bays for inspection: reconnoitring dump. 1 Section on 10 ton axle load bridge over BOSSUYT canal at O.2.b.98.40. No 4 relieved them at 1600 hrs. Road reconnaissance.	
	23rd		Forward road reconnaissance. No 2 Sectn & finally No 4 Section on bridge at O.2.b.98.40. Completed bridge 1800 hrs. No 1 Sectn continued listing dump stores.	
	24th		29th Div. relieved. Coy. remained in billets. Party on notice-boarding forward. Rest, refitting, & repairing baths installation at FACTORY I.20.c.6.2.	
	25th		Moved with 86th Bde group to NEUVILLE en FERRAIN area	
	26th		" " " " " BONDUES Sheet 36 E.23.a.1.4	
	27th		Kit inspection: & Company paid.	

(A9175) Wt W2358/P36 / 650,000 12/17 D. D. & L. Sch. 52a. Forms/C2118/15

Instructions regarding War Diaries and Intelligence Summaries are contained in F. S. Regs., Part II, and the Staff Manual respectively. Title pages will be prepared in manuscript.

WAR DIARY
or
~~INTELLIGENCE SUMMARY.~~
(Erase heading not required.)

Army Form C. 2118.

Place	Date	Hour	Summary of Events and Information	Remarks and references to Appendices
B.E.F. 28th	→		Re-allotted cycles – inspected tool-carts – sorted out harness etc.	
	29th		Moved to SCHOOL in CROIX. Lt COATES went on leave	
	30th		Work at 0700 with 10th Canadian Railway Company clearing demolished bridges L.8.c.7.0.	
	31st		Ditto.	

J. T. Godfrey Capt. R.E.
A/OC. 56th. Field Coy. R.E.

(A9175) Wt W2358/P36 600,000 12/17 D. D. & L. Sch. 52a. Forms/C2118/15

CONFIDENTIAL.

WAR DIARY

OF

510th (LONDON) FIELD COY. R.E.

FROM 1-11-18 TO 30-11-18.

VOLUME 29.

Volume 29.

1918.

Instructions regarding War Diaries and Intelligence Summaries are contained in F. S. Regs., Part II, and the Staff Manual respectively. Title pages will be prepared in manuscript.

WAR DIARY
or
INTELLIGENCE SUMMARY.
(*Erase heading not required.*)

Army Form C. 2118.

Place	Date	Hour	Summary of Events and Information	Remarks and references to Appendices
	November			
B.E.F.	1st		Repairing main railway in ~~Croix~~ CROIX	
	2nd		"	
	3rd		No work on railway. Refitting company	
	4th		Work on railway in CROIX	
	5th		"	
	6th		No work. Prepared to move	
	7th		Moved to TOURCOING.	
	8th		Moved to RUDERSVOORDE. Reconnoitred L'ESCAUT and GRAND COURANT	
	9th		Enemy retired from ESCAUT. Coy. moved to HELGHIN. Made two pack mule bridges over GRAND COURANT at Sheet 29. U.30.d.7.6. and V.20.a.7.5.	
	10th		Work on lorry bridge over GRAND COURANT and marshes at Sheet 37 C.5 b.5.4. with 14th Div. Engineers. Road repairs near CELLES. Reconnaissance of bridges over R. RHOSNES in Div. area.	
	11th		Coy. moved to Fme de la RHOSNES. Sheet 37. E.30. b.7.4. Work on bridge over RHOSNES at E.30. b.8.4 which was completed tonight. Hostilities ceased 11.00 hrs	
	12th		Reconnaissance.	

(A9175) Wt W2358/P36 600,000 12/17 D. D. & L. Sch. 52a. Forms/C2118/15.

Instructions regarding War Diaries and Intelligence Summaries are contained in F. S. Regs., Part II, and the Staff Manual respectively. Title pages will be prepared in manuscript.

1918

WAR DIARY
or
INTELLIGENCE SUMMARY.
(Erase heading not required.)

Army Form C. 2118.

Place	Date	Hour	Summary of Events and Information	Remarks and references to Appendices
	November			
BEF	13th		Road reconnaissance Commenced work on bridges at Sheet 37. F.19. c. 0.8. and E.18. b. 8.1	
	14th		Moved to FLOBECQ (Sheet TOURNAI 5)	
	15th } 16th } 17th }		Prepared for the march	
	18th		Moved to SILLY	
	19th, 20th		Rested.	
	21st		Moved to PICHAIN (Sheet BRUSSELS 6)	
	22nd		Rested	
	23rd		Moved to WITTERZEE	
	24th		Moved to COURT ST ÉTIENNE	
	25th		Moved to SART LES WALHAIN	
	26th		Rested	
	27th		Moved to TAVIERS	
	28th		Moved to ~~Antheit~~ ANTHEIT (Sheet LIEGE 7)	

Army Form C. 2118.

Instructions regarding War Diaries and Intelligence Summaries are contained in F. S. Regs., Part II. and the Staff Manual respectively. Title pages will be prepared in manuscript.

WAR DIARY
or
INTELLIGENCE SUMMARY.
(Erase heading not required.)

Place	Date	Hour	Summary of Events and Information	Remarks and references to Appendices
	Nov.			
B.E.F.	29th		Moved to ELLEMELLE (Sheet MARCHE 9).	
	~~30th~~		~~Stopped at ELLEMELLE and cleaned up Cy. wagons etc.~~ JG	
	30th		Moved to SOUGNE	
			J.A. Godfrey, Capt. RE	

(A9175) Wt W2358/P36 600,000 12/17 D. D. & L. Sch. 52a. Forms/C2118/15.

CONFIDENTIAL

WAR DIARY.

of

510th (LONDON) FIELD COY. R.E.

From 1-12-18 To 31-12-18

VOLUME No. 30

510th (LONDON) FIELD COY. RE

Instructions regarding War Diaries and Intelligence Summaries are contained in F. S. Regs., Part II, and the Staff Manual respectively. Title pages will be prepared in manuscript.

Volume 30.

WAR DIARY
or
INTELLIGENCE SUMMARY.
(Erase heading not required.)

Army Form C. 2118.

Place	Date	Hour	Summary of Events and Information	Remarks and references to Appendices
	Dec: 1918			
B.E.F.	1.		Company moved from SOUGNE to VERT BOUSSON	
	2		At VERT BOUSSON. Major KEAST returned from leave	
	3		Ditto Capt. GODFREY to Field Ambulance Sick	
	4		Company moved by Route March to BURNENVILLE - 15 Miles. Crossed German Frontier at 1445 Hours.	
	5		Company moved by Route March to WEISMES - 8 Miles	
	6		" " " " " MONTJOIE - 15½ "	
	7		" " " BERG - 21 " Surrey Staff ... Had to double Horse Wagons	
	8.		Company moved to ERP - 13 Miles. Following French Decoration awarded:- Major KEAST Croix de Guerre à l'ordre Corps. II Lieut COATES. Croix de Guerre à l'ordre Brigade II Cpl (a/Cpl) C WILLIAMS Croix de Guerre à l'ordre Regiment.	
	9		Company moved to SULZ COLOGNE Capt GODFREY rejoined from CCS	
	10		At SULZ Cleaning up Equipment - Major Harness etc Clipping Horses	
	11		Ditto Ditto Ditto Ditto	
	12		Ditto Ditto Ditto Ditto	[signature] Major RE

(A9175) Wt W2358/P56 600,000 12/17 D. D. & L. Sch. 52a. Forms/C2118/15

570th Field Coy. RE

Instructions regarding War Diaries and Intelligence Summaries are contained in F. S. Regs., Part II, and the Staff Manual respectively. Title pages will be prepared in manuscript.

Volume 30.
Sheet 2

WAR DIARY
or
~~INTELLIGENCE~~ SUMMARY.
(*Erase heading not required.*)

Army Form C. 2118.

Place	Date	Hour	Summary of Events and Information	Remarks and references to Appendices
	Dec. 1918			
B.E.F.	13.		Company moved by Route from SULZ to KAULE near BENSBERG. – II Army Commander inspected Division at W. end HOHENZOLLERN Bridge – COLOGNE as they marched past.	
	14		At KAULE. Company Parade – Cleaning Equipment – Making Notice Boards.	
	15		Ditto. Clipping Horses.	
	16		Ditto – Washing Tool Carts. Sharpening Tools etc.	
	17		Ditto – CAPT. GODFREY goes on Leave. To BURSCHEID with CRE re new billeting area. F.G.C.M. No 185786 Sapper MACKAY RE.	
	18		Company Parade – Sharpening Tools etc.	
	19		Company moved by Route March to BURSCHEID. All 3 Field Coys + H.Q. RE located at BURSCHEID.	
	20		BURSCHEID. Coy. Commanders Conference by CRE. F.G.C.M. on Sapper MACKAY. Promulgated.	
	21.		BURSCHEID. 1st Regtl. Guard mounted by 570th Field Coy. – Coy on Regtl Duty making Notice Boards + making Roadway at Horse Lines. Lt. MOFFET proceeds on Leave.	

J. Blackburn? Major RE

510th Field Coy. RE   Volume 30   Sheet 3

Army Form C. 2118.

WAR DIARY ~~or INTELLIGENCE~~ SUMMARY.

(*Erase heading not required.*)

Instructions regarding War Diaries and Intelligence Summaries are contained in F. S. Regs., Part II. and the Staff Manual respectively. Title pages will be prepared in manuscript.

Place	Date	Hour	Summary of Events and Information	Remarks and references to Appendices
	Dec. 18			
B.E.F.	22		BURSCHEID Company on Regt Duty – Making ... at Drivers Billets. Unloading Pontoons & Trestles & stacking under Cover. Clearing Wagons from Station Yard	
	23	Ditto	Coy on Regt Duty. Making Tempy Kitchens Sappers Billets etc. 11 Reinforcement Joined Coy	
	24	Ditto	Leave men rejoined Coy from MENIN – Road work Horse Lines	
	25	Ditto	Christmas Day – Church Parade only	
	26	Ditto	Preparing RE Workshops for starting Work – Parking Wagons under Cover – Road repairs	
	27	Ditto	Workshops Started –	
	28	Ditto	Whole Coy – less Workshops Party Unloading Train of RE Stores	
	29	Ditto	Party of 30. Unloading Train – Church Parade 1100	
	30	Ditto	Coy on Regt Duty – Stacking RE Stores	
	31	Ditto	Ditto Ditto	

S. Bartlett ... Major RE

(A9173) Wt W2353/P36 600,000 12/17 D. D. & L. Sch. 52a. Forms/C2118/15.

RHINE ARMY
SOUTHERN DIVISION
LATE 29TH DIVISION

510TH(LONDON) FLD COY R.E.

JAN - OCT 1919

2066 & 2084

C O N F I D E N T I A L

W A R D I A R Y.

of

510" FIELD COY RE

From 1/1/19 To 31/1/19

VOLUME No. 30

WO 31/29

510th (London) Field Coy. R.E.

VOLUME 31

JANUARY 1919

Instructions regarding War Diaries and Intelligence Summaries are contained in F. S. Regs., Part II, and the Staff Manual respectively. Title pages will be prepared in manuscript.

WAR DIARY or INTELLIGENCE SUMMARY.

(Erase heading not required.)

Army Form C. 2118.

Place	Date	Hour	Summary of Events and Information	Remarks and references to Appendices
	1919.			
BURSCHEID	Jan. 1.		2 Secn at R.E. Dump - Stacking Stores - Remainder R.E. Workshops.	
GERMANY	2.		Ditto.	
	3		Ditto - Stacking Stores - 1 Secn on Coy. Stables - Remainder Workshops.	
	4.		Ditto	
	5.		Sunday. Church Parade	
	6.		No 1 & 2 Secn (part of) Felling trees for Stable Poles etc. 1 Secn on Coy. Billets - Remainder Workshops.	
	7		Ditto - Educational Scheme Started - First Class Held	
	8		Ditto 22 Infantry for Sectional Instn arrived & billetted & fed with Coy	
	9		CRE inspection Horses & Harness. - Workshops Party - Balance Nos 1 & 2 Secn	
			Started ASC Stables - KALTERHERBERG Remainder Coy. Stables & Billets	
	10		Ditto Lt MEFFET returned from Leave	
	11		Ditto. Reconnaissance of area allotted to 510th F. Coy. Started	
	12		Sunday Church Parade	
	13.		Workshops - Balance 1 & 2 Secn ASC Stables - Balance No 3 Secn Started Bunking	
			at New Drivers Billets - Balance No 4 Secn Bunking - Kitchen - Ablution Shed - Sappers Billets	
	14		Ditto	

(A9175) Wt W2358/P361 600,000 12/17 D. D. & L. Sch. 52a. Forms/C2118/15.

[signature]

510th (London) Field Coy. R.E. Volume 31 Contd. 2

Army Form C. 2118.

Instructions regarding War Diaries and Intelligence Summaries are contained in F. S. Regs., Part II. and the Staff Manual respectively. Title pages will be prepared in manuscript.

WAR DIARY
or
INTELLIGENCE SUMMARY.
(Erase heading not required.)

Place	Date 1919	Hour	Summary of Events and Information	Remarks and references to Appendices
BURSCHEID	Jan. 15th		As per 14th	
GERMANY	16		Ditto - Capt. GODFREY R.E. returned from leave.	
	17		Ditto	
	18		Drill Parade & Barrack Cleaning - Capt. Godfrey D.V.K. for course	
	19		Sunday. Church Parade	
	20		Workshops - A.S.C. Stables KALTER HERBERG - Drivers & Sappers Billets Bunking etc	
	21		Ditto	
	22		Ditto Major Reed to Medical Board - 21. Infy. Carpenters arrived for Instruction	
	23		Ditto Workshop Ex'n started	
	24		Ditto	
	25		Drill Parade & Barrack Cleaning	
	26		Sunday - Church Parade	
	27		As per 24th	
	28		Ditto	
	29		Ditto	
	30		Ditto	
	31		Ditto	

S. Bush Reed
Major R.E.

WO 32

WAR DIARY

OF

510TH (LONDON) FIELD COY. R.E.

VOLUME 32

FROM 1-2-19 TO 28-2-19.

510th (LONDON) Field Coy: RE

Instructions regarding War Diaries and Intelligence Summaries are contained in F. S. Regs., Part II. and the Staff Manual respectively. Title pages will be prepared in manuscript.

Volume 32

WAR DIARY
or
INTELLIGENCE SUMMARY.
(Erase heading not required.)

Army Form C. 2118.

Place	Date	Hour	Summary of Events and Information	Remarks and references to Appendices
	Feb: 1919			
BURSCHEID	1.		Coy & Regt: Ceremonial Parades - practice for G.O.C's Inspection	
GERMANY	2.		Sunday. Barrack Cleaning - Wagon - Harness & Equipment cleaning	
	3.		G.O.C's Inspection. Medals Ribbons presented to Far: Sergt: BURR. M.S.M. Corpl: Parsons. M.M. - Major Kear. 2nd Lt Coates - Corpl Williams - Medals Croix de Guerre (French) 2nd Corpl Strand - Lce Cpl Oxford - Ribbons - Croix de Guerre - (Belgian)	
	4		Workshops & ASC Stables Kattenberg - Drivers Billets.	
	5.		Ditto	
	6		Ditto Lieut. Meffet to ORS.	
	7		Ditto Lt Col. Spedding - RA - to Classify Horses	
	8.		Route March - Barrack Cleaning. 2nd Lieut Coates & 28 ORs left for Demobilisation	
	9.		Church Parade	
	10.		Coy: Dismounted Portion organized into HQ & 1 & 2 Sections. No 1 Sect: (Works) a) ASC Stables KALTERHERBERG (b) HQ RE Kitchen (c) Coy. Stables No 2 " Workshops.	

(A9175) Wt W2358/P361 600,000 12/17 D. D. & L. Sch. 52a. Forms/C2118/15.

S Banks Kear Major RE

Sheet 2

Instructions regarding War Diaries and Intelligence Summaries are contained in F. S. Regs., Part II, and the Staff Manual respectively. Title pages will be prepared in manuscript.

WAR DIARY
or
~~INTELLIGENCE SUMMARY.~~
(Erase heading not required.)

Army Form C. 2118.

Place	Date	Hour	Summary of Events and Information	Remarks and references to Appendices
	Feb.	1919		
BURSCHEID	11.		As for 10th	
GERMANY	12		" " 11th plus - Boxing Rink for 87th Bde started	
	13.		" " 12th plus C.Q.M.S. whole Store enclosed.	
	14		" " 13th	
	15		Rifle Inspection Baths. + Barrack Cleaning	
	16		Church Parade	
	17.		New Coy. Stables Commenced.	
	18.		New Coy Stables - ASC Stables. + Workshops	
	19		Ditto. Stables for 1st BORDER at HILGEN Commenced	
	20.		As for 19th 20. Y+Z Animals to 29th DAC for Mallein Test.	
	21.		As for 20th - Baths.	
	22nd.		Rifle Inspection. Works as for 20th. Barrack Cleaning - 2/Lt CHILVERS joined	
	23.		Church Parade	
	24		Works as for 22nd. No.1 Sect. New Coy. Stables - ASC Stables No.2 Sect Workshops & Stables at HILGEN	
	25		As for 24th MAJOR MURNANE arrived to take over Company	[initials]

(A9175) Wt W2358/P36 650,000 12/17 D. D. & L. Sch. 52a. Forms/C2118/15.

Sheet 3

Instructions regarding War Diaries and Intelligence Summaries are contained in F. S. Regs., Part II. and the Staff Manual respectively. Title pages will be prepared in manuscript.

WAR DIARY
or
INTELLIGENCE SUMMARY.
(Erase heading not required.)

Army Form C. 2118.

Place	Date	Hour	Summary of Events and Information	Remarks and references to Appendices
	Feb.	1919		
BURSCHEID	26.		Work as for 25th Major Keast handing over Company to Major Murnane	S Banks Keast Major RE
GERMANY	27.		Ditto. Ditto. Major Keast leaves for England	
"	28		ditto	
"	29			

D J Murnane Major RE

(A9175) Wt W2358/P361 500,000 12/17 D. D. & L. Sch. 52a. Forms/C2118/15.

29th Div.

CONFIDENTIAL

WAR DIARY.

of

510th LONDON FIELD COY. R.E

From MAY 1st To MAY 31st

VOLUME No 35

J. Kendall MAJOR, R.E
O.C. 510th (LONDON) FIELD COY R.E.

MAY 1919.

WAR DIARY of 510th FIELD Coy RE.
or
INTELLIGENCE SUMMARY.
(Erase heading not required.)

VOLUME No35
Army Form C. 2118.

Instructions regarding War Diaries and Intelligence Summaries are contained in F. S. Regs., Part II. and the Staff Manual respectively. Title pages will be prepared in manuscript.

Place	Date	Hour	Summary of Events and Information	Remarks and references to Appendices
	1.5.19		Coy engaged on work. Stables for RFA at WHITZHELDEN. Huts for drivers of Coy billets ~~or~~ Instructing battalion pioneers & running workshops.	[initials]
	2.5.19		work as usual	[initials]
	3.5.19		Training in rifle exercises etc & gas drill	[initials]
	4.5.19		Church Parades	[initials]
	5.5.19 – 9.5.19		work as usual	[initials]
	10.5.19		Training gas drill & baths.	[initials]
	11.5.19		Church Parades	[initials]
	12.5.19 – 16.5.19		work as usual	[initials]
	17.5.19		2nd class of Infantry battalion pioneers returned to unit. 2 class of Pioneer battalion returned to unit.	[initials]
	18.5.19		Church parades.	[initials]
	19.5.19		3 class of Infantry battalion pioneers reported for course in woodwork & erection of small huts (i.e.) cookhouses latrines sheds etc. all men shown how to build field kitchens. 24 OR of 9th Gloucesters attached for work to replace german labour. Work as usual	[initials]

(A9175) Wt W2353/P36 600,000 12/17 D. D. & L. Sch. 52a. Forms/C2118/15.

Instructions regarding War Diaries and Intelligence Summaries are contained in F. S. Regs., Part II, and the Staff Manual respectively. Title pages will be prepared in manuscript.

MAY 1919.

WAR DIARY of 510 Field Coy R E.
or
INTELLIGENCE SUMMARY.
(*Erase heading not required.*)

VOLUME No 35
Army Form C. 2118.

Place	Date	Hour	Summary of Events and Information	Remarks and references to Appendices
	20.5.19		work as usual.	[initials]
	21.5.19.		work commenced on Disinfestor at LEICHLINGEN.	[initials]
	22.5.19		" " on Gun Park for RFA. WHITZHELDEN	[initials]
	25.5.19		Church Parades	[initials]
	26.5.19		workshops inspected by Commander in Cheif.	[initials]
	28.5.19		work at stables at WHITZHELDEN completed	[initials]
	29.5.19		work commenced on disinfestor at BURSCHEID.	[initials]

J Kendall [signature]
O.C. 510 (LONDON) FIELD COY. R.E.

(A9575) Wt W2358/P36 6,0,000 12/17 D. D. & L. Sch. 52a. Forms C2118/15.

29 DIV

Southern

CONFIDETIAL

WAR DIARY FOR JUNE

510 LONDON FIELD COY. R.E.

VOLUME No 36

MAJOR

O.C. 510th (LONDON) FIELD COY

Instructions regarding War Diaries and Intelligence Summaries are contained in F. S. Regs., Part II. and the Staff Manual respectively. Title pages will be prepared in manuscript.

JUNE 1919. **WAR DIARY** *or* **INTELLIGENCE SUMMARY.** OF 510th FIELD Coy RE VOLUME 36

(Erase heading not required.)

Army Form C. 2118.

Place	Date	Hour	Summary of Events and Information	Remarks and references to Appendices
BURSCHEID	1·6·19	.	Lt J A BELILE joined the Coy. Coy engaged in baths & drainage	[illegible]
Germany	2·6·19		Church parades.	[illegible]
	3·6·19		One officer & 25 O.R. formed part of RE detachment on Kings birthday parade. Inspected by Corps Commander.	[illegible]
	4·6·19 – 5·6·19		Work as usual.	[illegible]
	6·6·19 – 7·6·19		Divisional races. Half company at races each day	[illegible]
	8·6·19		Church parades.	[illegible]
	9·6·19		Whit monday. General holiday.	[illegible]
	10·6·19 – 12·6·19		Work as usual. Work on stables	[illegible]
	13·6·19		at WALD HELDEN completed. 3rd Infantry Batt. [illegible] course completed & men returned to units.	[illegible]
	15·6·19		Church Parades.	[illegible]
	16·6·19		Orders received to prepare for advance in event of peace terms not being signed.	[illegible]
	17·6·19		Men recalled from detachment. Surplus ordnance stores returned to [illegible] MOLHEIM. 2 sections & 1 Transport [illegible] sent to 2nd Infantry Bde. during H[illegible]GEN.	

(A9175) Wt W2358/P361 6,0,000 12/17 D. D. & L. Sch. 52a. Forms/C2118/15

Instructions regarding War Diaries and Intelligence Summaries are contained in F. S. Regs., Part II, and the Staff Manual respectively. Title pages will be prepared in manuscript.

VOLUME 36

Army Form C. 2118.

JUNE 1919. WAR DIARY of 510 Field Coy R.E. or INTELLIGENCE SUMMARY.

(Erase heading not required.)

Place	Date	Hour	Summary of Events and Information	Remarks and references to Appendices
BURSCHEID Germany	18.6.19 to 20.6.19		Packing wagons & removing stores to Dump. Company ready to move at an hours notice	[initials]
	21.6.19		Short route march	[initials]
	22.6.19 to 27.6.19		Preparing for C.R.E's inspection. No work continued outside BURSCHEID	[initials]
	28.6.19		C R Es inspection Peace signed	[initials]
	29.6.19		Church parades.	[initials]

[signature] Wendall.

MAJOR, R.E.
O.C. 510 FIELD COY. R.E.

(A9275) Wt W2358/P36 6,0,000 12/17 D. D. & L. Sch. 52a. Forms/C2118/15.

CONFIDENTIAL

SERIAL Nö 3.7.

WAR DIARY of

510th LONDON FIELD COMPANY R.E.

[signature] Major R.E.
O.C.510 London Field Coy.R.E.

Instructions regarding War Diaries and Intelligence Summaries are contained in F. S. Regs., Part II. and the Staff Manual respectively. Title pages will be prepared in manuscript.

JULY 1919 WAR DIARY OF 510 FIELD COY RE
or
~~INTELLIGENCE SUMMARY~~.
(Erase heading not required.)

Army Form C. 2118.

VOLUME 37

Place	Date	Hour	Summary of Events and Information	Remarks and references to Appendices
BURSCHEID GERMANY	1.7.19.		Work resumed on Disinfestor LEICHLINGEN.	[initials]
	2.7.19		work as usual in workshops & Disinfestor for Burscheid;	[initials]
	3.7.19		Large meat stores for RASC at KALTERNHERBURG. cookhouse for RE camp Burscheid	[initials]
	4.7.19		General holiday to celebrate peace.	[initials]
	6.7.19		Church parades.	[initials]
	7.7.19 to 11.7.19		work as usual.	[initials]
	13.7.19		Church parades.	[initials]
	14.7.19		work as usual.	[initials]
	15.7.19		Lt GARBUTT MC RE & 2 OR on detachment preparing ground of Southern DW Tournament.	[initials]
	20.7.19		Church parades	[initials]
	21.7.19–25.7.19		work as usual.	[initials]
	28.7.19.		Lt GARBUTT MC RE left for England on demobilisation	[initials]

(A9175) Wt W2358/P56 600,000 12/7 D. D. & L. Sch. 52a. Forms/C2118/15.

C O N F I D E N T I A L

SERIAL No 38

W A R D I A R Y of

510th LONDON FIELD COMPANY R.E.
+++++++++++++++++++++++++++++++++

[signature], Major R.E.
O.C.510 London Field Coy.R.E.

VOLUME Nº. 38.

Army Form C. 2118.

AUGUST 1919 **WAR DIARY** OF 510 FIELD COY RE.

or

INTELLIGENCE SUMMARY.

(Erase heading not required.)

Instructions regarding War Diaries and Intelligence Summaries are contained in F. S. Regs., Part II. and the Staff Manual respectively. Title pages will be prepared in manuscript.

Place	Date	Hour	Summary of Events and Information	Remarks and references to Appendices
BURSCHEID	1.8.19.		Work as usual. Coy engaged on erecting Disinfectors at LEICHLINGHAM and BURSCHEID. Storage sapes for RASC at KALTERN HERBURG & WERMLESKERTION. Running workshops at BURSCHEID.	R
	3.8.19		Church parades	R
	7.8.19		Disinfector at LEICHLINGHAM & storage sape at KALTERN HERBURG complete	R
	21.8.19.		Disinfector at BURSCHEID & storage sape at WERMLESKERTION complete.	R
	27.8.19.		LT ELTOFT RE left for EGYPT.	
			Draft 1 NCO & 2 OR left for EGYPT on 15.8.19. 4 men demobilised during the month.	R

[signature]
MAJOR, R.E.
O.C. 510 FIELD COY R.E.

(A9295) Wt W2338/P36 · 6,0,000 12/17 D. D. & L. Sch. 52a. Forms/C2118/15.

C O N F I D E N T I A L

SERIAL No 39.

W A R D I A R Y of 520-1

510th LONDON FIELD COMPANY R.E.
++++++++++++++++++++++++++++++++++

J Kendall . Major R.E.
O.C. 510 London Field Coy. R.E.

VOLUME 39

SEPTEMBER 1919.

Instructions regarding War Diaries and Intelligence Summaries are contained in F. S. Regs., Part II. and the Staff Manual respectively. Title pages will be prepared in manuscript.

WAR DIARY OF 510 FIELD COY RE or ~~INTELLIGENCE SUMMARY.~~

Army Form C. 2118.

(Erase heading not required.)

Place	Date	Hour	Summary of Events and Information	Remarks and references to Appendices
BURSCHEID	1-9-19		Coy engaged on ablution house at WERMELSKIRCHEN for 100 men. Camp improvements & running workshops.	
	2-9-19		MAJOR KENDALL MC RE granted leave to U.K. Capt SEYMOUR assumed command of Coy. 2/Lt CHILVERS RE attached to 126 Bde RHA for instruction	
	8-9-19		4 O.R. left unit for Egyptian draft.	
	12-9-19		Lt BARKER SIMSON RE transferred to 497 Field Coy RE	
	13-9-19		work at WERMELSKIRCHEN complete. owing to demobilisation all work ceases.	
	16-9-19		MAJOR KENDALL MC RE rejoined unit from leave & assumed command of Coy.	
	18-9-19		Capt Seymour RE granted leave to U.K.	
	27-9-19		All leave + demobilisation stopped owing to Railway strike	
	27-9-19		MAJOR KENDALL MC RE acting C.R.E.	
	-30-9-19		During month 63 O.R demobilised & 14 horses.	

M Kendall
MAJOR, R.E.
O.C. 510th. (LONDON) FIELD COY. R.E.

(A0175) Wt W2358/P36 600,000 12/17 D. D. & L. Sch. 52a. Forms/C2118/15

C O N F I D E N T I A L

SERIAL Nō 40

W A R D I A R Y of

510th LONDON FIELD COMPANY R.E.
++ +++++++++++++++++++++++++++++++++

Major R.E.

O.C. 510 Londo Field Coy. R.E.

VOLUME 40

Army Form C. 2118.

WAR DIARY or INTELLIGENCE SUMMARY. OF 510 FIELD Coy R.E.

OCTOBER 1919

Instructions regarding War Diaries and Intelligence Summaries are contained in F. S. Regs., Part II. and the Staff Manual respectively. Title pages will be prepared in manuscript.

(*Erase heading not required.*)

Place	Date	Hour	Summary of Events and Information	Remarks and references to Appendices
BURSCHEID	1.10.19		Coy engaged on cleaning & checking coy equipment. Demobilisation held up owing to railway strike in England.	R
	10.10.19		Demob opened strike settled	R
	14.10.19		Capt Seymour rejoined from leave	R
	17.10.19		16 mules sent away for sale.	R
	25.10.19		17 horses & 17 mules sent away.	R
	24.10.19		All equipment & vehicles stored in Factory at MULHEIM. All tools etc to be packed in cases for dispatch for England.	R
	27.10.19		All coy less OC & 6 O.R. proceeded to join 206 Field Coy R.E.	R
	28.10.19		OC & 6 O.R. proceeded to MULHEIM. to complete packing of stores	R

[signature]

MAJOR, R.E.
O.C. 510th (LONDON) FIELD COY. R.E.

www.ingramcontent.com/pod-product-compliance
Lightning Source LLC
Chambersburg PA
CBHW081525160426
43191CB00011B/1682
* 9 7 8 1 4 7 4 5 1 4 6 0 6 *